ILLUSTRATED ATLAS
--OF--
SHIAWASSEE COUNTY
1895
--MICHIGAN--

ILLUSTRATED

ATLAS

OF

SHIAWASSEE COUNTY

MICHIGAN

Compiled and Published from Recent Surveys, Official Records, and Personal Examinations

INCLUDING BRIEF BIOGRAPHICAL SKETCHES OF
ENTERPRISING CITIZENS

THE ATLAS PUBLISHING COMPANY
BATTLE CREEK, MICHIGAN
1895

ENGRAVED AND PRINTED BY THE REVIEW AND HERALD PUB. CO., BATTLE CREEK, MICH.

TABLE OF CONTENTS.

TOWNSHIP MAPS.

STATE, COUNTY, CITY, AND VILLAGE MAPS.

ILLUSTRATIONS.

County Buildings.
Group of Owosso Churches.
Maple Ridge Park, Owosso.
Portraits and Residence of John Reed and wife, of Vernon Township.

Residence of Mrs. Jane White, of Vernon Township.
The Lennon Elevator, Property of Geo. F. Denham, Lennon.
Members of Shiawassee County Bar.
Group of County Officials.

EXPLANATIONS.

Railroads in Operation.
Street Railway Lines.
Township Lines.
Corporation Lines.
Section Lines.
Quarter Section Lines.
Farm Lines.

Ward Boundary.
Distance on Wagon Roads between Branches.
Important Dates.
Rivers.
Unfillable Land.
School District Boundary.
Section Numbers.
Area of Farms.

OUTLINE MAP

OF

SHIAWASSEE COUNTY, MICHIGAN.

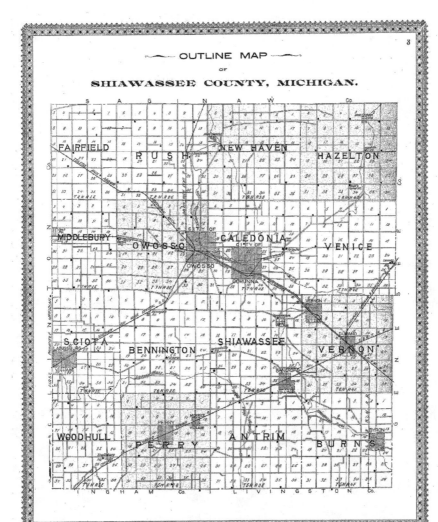

MAP OF
FAIRFIELD

Township 8 North   Range 1 East

Scale, 2 Inches to the Mile

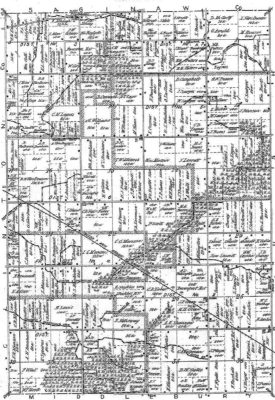

MAP OF
· RUSH ·

Township 8 North   Range 2 East

Scale, 2 inches to the Mile

MAP OF
NEW HAVEN

Township 8 North   Range 3 East

Scale, 2 Inches to the Mile

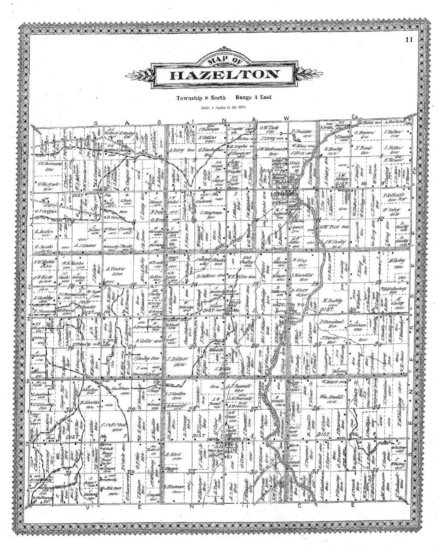

MAP OF
HAZELTON

Township 8 North   Range 4 East

Scale, 1 Inches to the Mile

MAP OF
MIDDLEBURY

Township 7 North Range 1 East

Scale, 2 Inches to the Mile

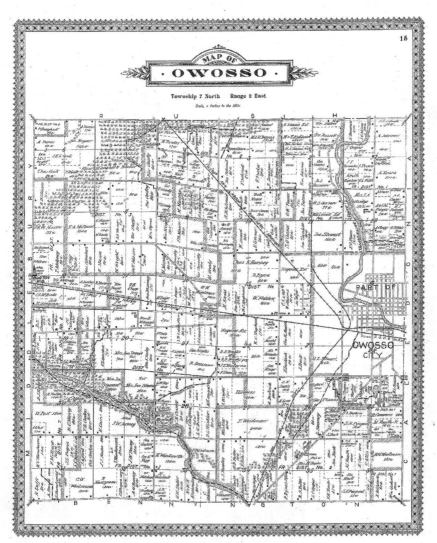

MAP OF
· OWOSSO ·

Township 7 North   Range 2 East

Scale, 2 Inches to the Mile

MAP OF
CALEDONIA

Township 7 North   Range 3 East

Scale, 2 Inches to the Mile

MAP OF
VENICE

Township 7 North   Range 4 East

Scale, 2 Inches to the Mile

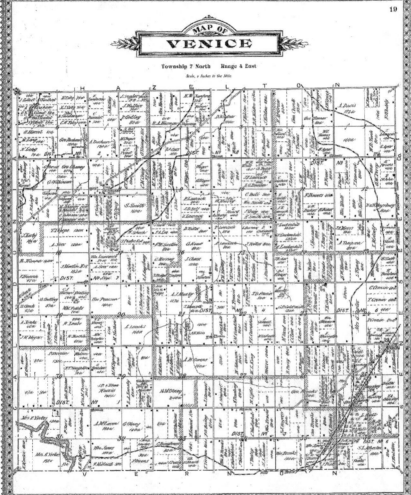

MAP OF
SCIOTA

Township 6 North   Range 1 East

Scale, 2 Inches to the Mile.

MAP OF
BENNINGTON

Township 6 North   Range 2 East

Scale, 2 Inches to the Mile

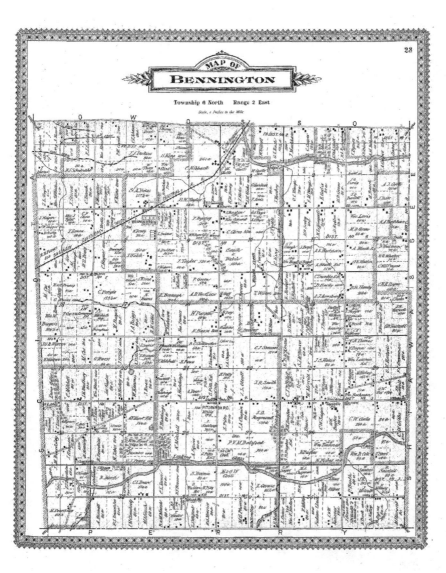

MAP OF
SHIAWASSEE

Township 6 North   Range 3 East

Scale, ¾ Inches to the Mile

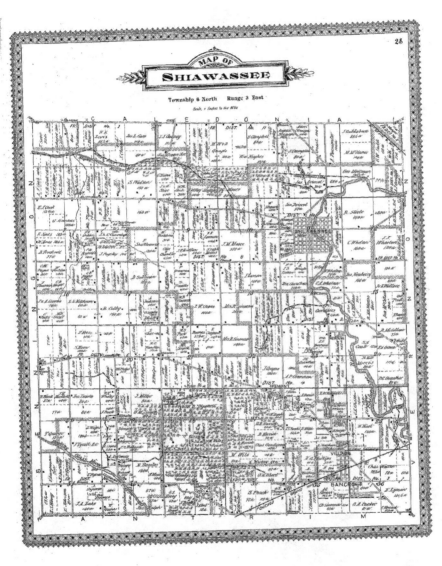

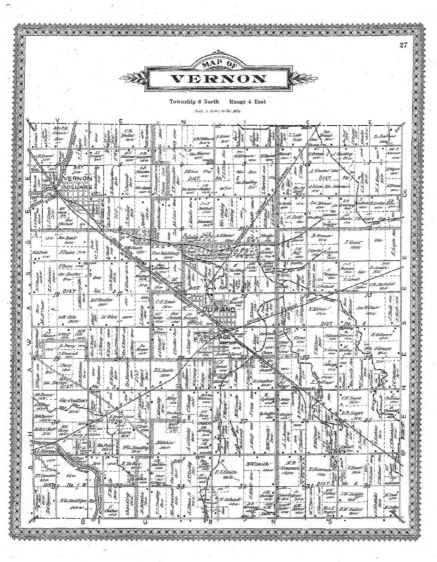

MAP OF
VERNON

Township 6 North   Range 4 East

Scale, 2 Inches to the Mile

MAP OF WOODHULL

Township 5 North   Range 1 East

Scale, 2 Inches to the Mile

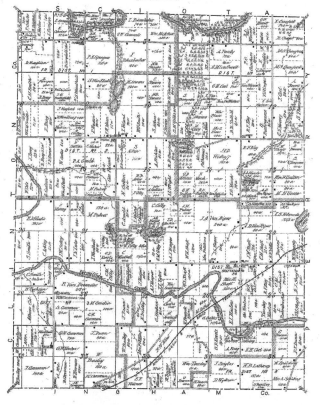

· PERRY ·

Township 6 North   Range 2 East

Scale, 2 Inches to the Mile

BENNINGTON

INGHAM   Co.

MAP OF
ANTRIM

Township 5 North   Range 3 East

Scale, 2 Inches to the Mile

S H I A W A S S E E

L I V I N G S T O N   Co.

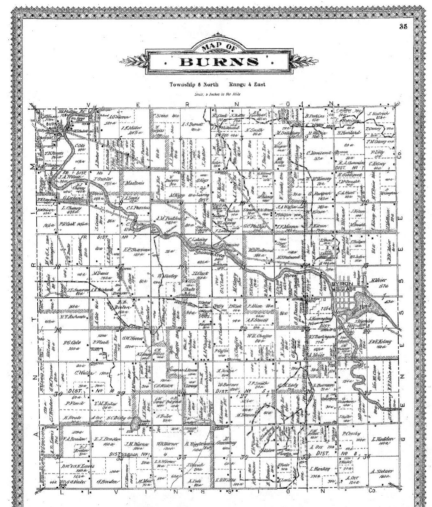

MAP OF
· BURNS ·

Township 6 North   Range 4 East

Scale, 2 Inches to the Mile

MABBIT'S ADDITION
OVID TO VILLAGE
MIDDLEBURY TP.

LENNON
VENICE TP.

MORRICE
PERRY TP.

HENDERSONVILLE
HENDERSON P.O.
RUSH TP.

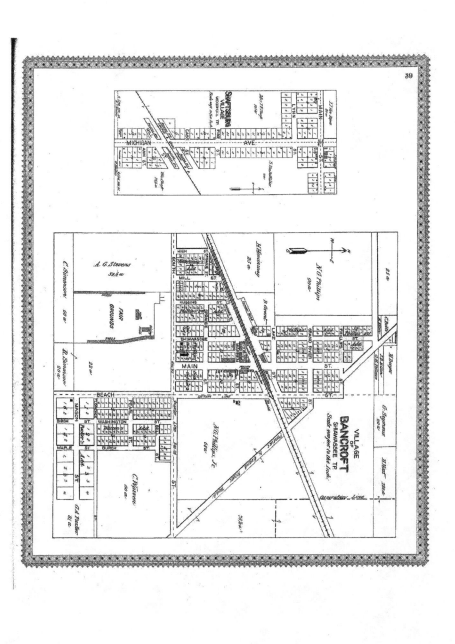

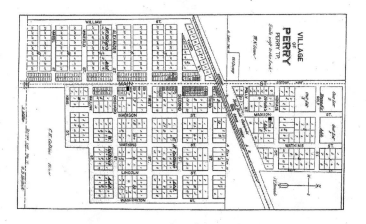

43

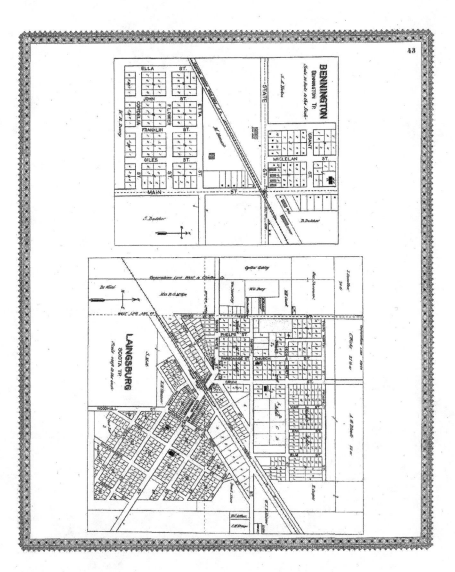

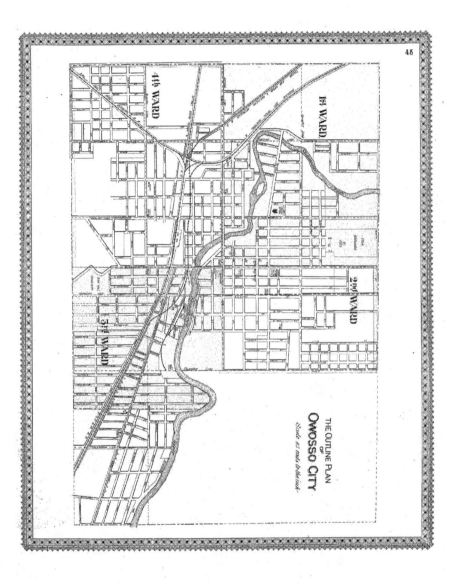

THE OUTLINE PLAN
OF
OWOSSO CITY

Scale 65 rods to the inch.

1st WARD

2nd WARD

3rd WARD

4th WARD

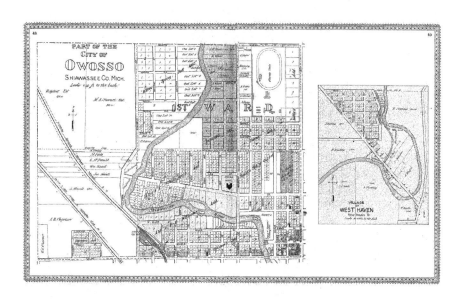

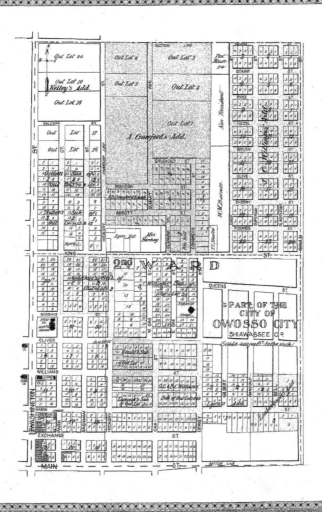

PART OF THE
CITY OF
OWOSSO CITY
SHIAWASSEE CO.

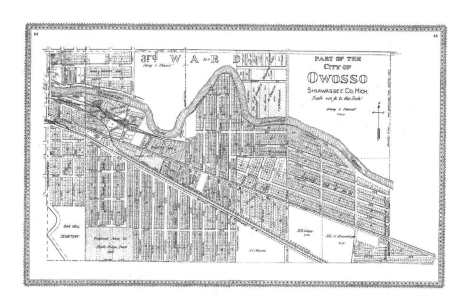

PART OF THE
CITY OF
OWOSSO
SHIAWASSEE CO. MICH.

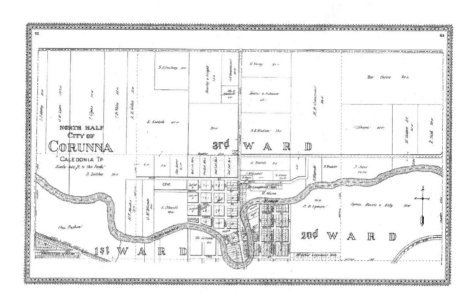

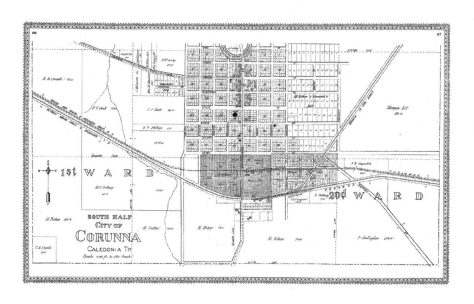

SOUTH HALF
CITY OF
CORUNNA
CALEDONIA TP.

1ST W A R D

2nd W A R D

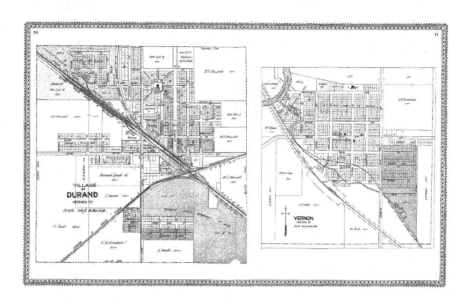

VILLAGE
OF
DURAND
VERNON TP.

VERNON
VERNON TP.

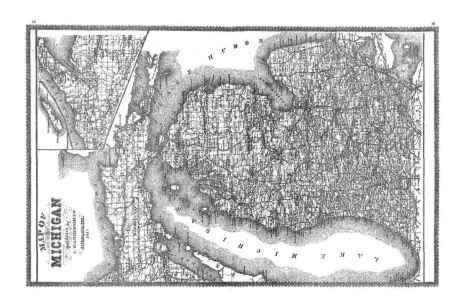

MAP OF
MICHIGAN
Published by
S. VANDERBILT
& CO BROOKLYN
1873

OFFICIAL REGISTER

— OF —

SHIAWASSEE COUNTY, MICHIGAN,

SHOWING

COUNTY AND COURT OFFICERS AND YEARS
OF SERVICE OF EACH.

COUNTY CLERKS.

Andrew Parsons	1837-1838
Ira B. Howard	1838-1840
John K. Smith	1840-1842
Joseph Purdy	1842-1848
Ebenezer F. Wade	1848-1852
Elias Comstock	1852-1854
Cortes Pond	1854-1856
Elias Comstock	1856-1860
George C. Holmes	1860-1864
Philip W. Coleman	1866-1868
John B. Graham	1868-1874
Almon G. Brown	1874-1878
Newton Baldwin	1878-1880
Frank E. Welch	1880-1888
Lester J. Kenney	1888-1890
Abram L. Board	1890-1892
Duane C. Cooper	1892-

COUNTY DRAIN COMMISSIONERS.

George T. Mason	1858-1889
Andrew Huggins	1889-1891
George T. Mason	1891-

COUNTY SUPERINTENDENT OF
SCHOOLS.

Ezekiel J. Cock	1870-

SECRETARY OF COUNTY BOARD
OF EXAMINERS.

James M. McBride	1889-1890
Henry B. Dewey	1890-1891

COUNTY COMMISSIONERS OF
SCHOOLS.

Hudson Sheldon	1891-1893
E. D. Dimond	1893-

STATE SENATORS.

Sanford M. Green	1843-1846
Andrew Parsons	1843-1851
Amos Gould	1852-1860
John N. Ingersoll	1860-1863
Hugh McCurdy	1865-1868
Jerome W. Turner	1868-1872
James M. Goodell	1872-1876
Lorison J. Taylor	1876-1878
Horace Halbert	1878-1880
Wm. M. Kilpatrick	1880-1882
Charles M. Wood	1882-1884
Henry H. Pulver	1884-1886
John Dollarck	1886-1890
Marcus Wilcox	1890-1892
Marshall E. Rumsey	1892-1894
Wm. M. Kilpatrick	1894-

SHERIFFS.

Levi Rowe	1837-1838
Elisha Brewster	1838-1842
David Bush	1842-1844
Elisha Brewster	1844-1848
Alonzo Howard	1848-1852
John M. Fitch	1852-1856
William P. Laing	1856-1860
Josiah Fuller	1860-1864

Seymour Shipman	1864-1866
David Parker	1866-1870
Andrew G. Kelso	1870-1872
Ferry B. Swain	1872-1874
Andrew G. Kelso	1874-1878
Clark D. Smith	1878-1882
Andrew G. Kelso	1882-1884
Wm. H. Cole	1884-1888
Francis G. Morris	1888-1892
William E. Jacobs	1892-

PROSECUTING ATTORNEYS.

Sanford M. Green	1837-1842
J. C. Smith	1843-1844
William P. Mosley	1844-1847
Andrew Parsons	1845-1847
William P. Mosley	1847-1849
Amos Gould	1849-1850
Richard B. Hall	1850-1852
Luke H. Parsons	1852-1854
William P. Mosley	1854-1856
Hugh McCurdy	1856-1858
S. Titus Parsons	1858-1860
Spencer B. Raynole	1860-1862
Benton Hanchett	1862-1864
James M. Goodell	1864-1866
Ebenezer Gould	1868-1868
James M. Goodell	1868-1870
Spencer B. Raynole	1870-1872
S. Titus Parsons	1872-1874
Hugh McCurdy	1874-1876
William M. Kilpatrick	1876-1880
Albert R. McBride	1880-1884
Stearns P. Smith	1884-1888
Selden S. Miner	1888-1892
Frank H. Watson	1892-

CIRCUIT COURT COMMISSIONERS.

Ebenezer Gould	1852-1856
Samuel T. Parsons	1852-1858
George K. Newcombe	1858-1860
Gilbert R. Lyon	1860-1864
Henry M. Newcombe	1864-1866
James M. Goodell	1866-1868
Hiram E. Chipman	1868-1870
K. Bonner Wyles	1870-1872
Lucius E. Gould	1872-1874
Curtis J. Gale	1874-1876
James G. Miller	1876-1878
Selden S. Miner	1878-1880
Lucius E. Gould	1880-1882
Selden S. Miner	1880-1882
Frank H. Watson	1882-1884
Chas. H. Hotchkiss	1882-1884
Frank H. Watson	1884-1886
Martin B. Wixom	1884-1886
Curtis J. Gale	1886-1890
Lucius E. Gould	1886-1890
Austine E. Richards	1890-1892
Newton Baldwin	1890-1892
Jonathan G. Knight	1892-
Frank P. Bump	1892-

CORONERS.

David H. Tyler	1838-1840
Ephraim H. Utley	1838-1840
John Woodruff	1840-1844

Lyman Melvin	1840-1844
Henry Leach	1844-1846
George Harrington	1844-1846
Horace B. Flint	1846-1848
Eliphalet B. Tooker	1846-1848
Aaron Swain	1848-1850
Henry Leach	1848-1850
George Harrington	1850-1852
Levi Rowe	1850-1852
Humphrey Wheeler	1852-1854
Joseph Howe	1852-1854
Humphrey Wheeler	1854-1856
Parmer C. Card	1854-1856
William E. Eddy	1856-1858
David Ingersoll	1856-1858
Jonah Fuller	1858-1860
Eli D. Gregory	1858-1860
Enoch Bally	1860-1862
James Garrison	1860-1862
George L. Hitchcock	1862-1864
James Garrison	1862-1864
Gazzy Tuttle	1864-1866
Tolman Warren	1864-1866
S. S. Marshall	1866-1870
Miles Tuttle	1866-1870
H. M. Marshall	1870-1872
George T. Swinn	1870-1872
Benjamin F. Taylor	1872-1878
Wells B. Fox	1872-1876
John L. Miller	1876-1878
Ezra M. Harvey	1878-1880
John L. Miller	1878-1880
Benjamin F. Taylor	1880-1882
John L. Miller	1880-1882
Bert C. Sickles	1882-1884
Erastus H. Knapp	1882-1884
Myron C. Scalley	1884-1886
Andrew Love	1884-1886
Albert A. Frain	1886-1888
Wm. P. Stedman	1886-1888
A. Frank Westcott	1888-1890
Benjamin S. Retan	1888-1890
James Sheth	1890-1892
George W. Crouch	1890-1892
George W. Crouch	1892-1894
Hiram Monroe	1892-1894
Hiram Monroe	1894-
A. T. Holcomb	1894-

REGISTERS OF DEEDS.

John M. Gilbert	1838-1840
Andrew Parsons	1840-1840
Luke H. Parsons	1840-1848
James E. Chaffee	1848-1852
Owen Corcoran	1852-1856
George W. Goodell	1856-1858
Chauncey S. Chaavers	1858-1861
William Oakes	1864-1866
Charles Holman	1866-1880
Nathaniel A. Finch	1880-1888
Wm. H. Bigelow	1888-

REPRESENTATIVES IN THE LEGIS-
LATURE.

Robert G. McKee	1838-1839
Lemuel Castle	1839-1842
Francis J. Prevost	1843-1844

Robert R. Tompson	1844-1847
Kustuter B. Martin	1847-1848
Herman G. Noble	1848-1850
Ebenezer C. Kimberly	1850-1852
Nicholas Gulick	1852-1854
Andrew Parsons	1854-1856
Dr. Charles P. Parkill	1856-1858
Sullivan R. Kelsey	1858-1862
Paul C. Sprague	1862-1864
S. Titus Parsons	1862-1864
William F. Laing	1864-1866
Nathan G. Phillips	1864-1866
S. Titus Parsons	1866-1868
Charles Locke	1866-1868
John N. Ingersoll	1868-1870
Edgar B. Ward	1868-1870
William D. Gartison	1870-1872
Charles V. Osburne	1870-1872
Frederick G. Bailey	1872-1874
Benjamin Walker	1872-1874
Frederick G. Bailey	1874-1876
Lorison J. Taylor	1874-1876
Rasselas Reed	1876-1880
Darwin W. Sharts	1876-1880
George H. Cooper	1880-1882
John W. Dewey	1880-1882
Fordyce H. Potter	1884-1884
Lawrence Van Dusen	1882-1884
Fordyce H. Potter	1884-1886
Chas. H. Cossitt	1884-1886
Worden R. Chapell	1884-1888
Frank H. Watson	1886-1888
Jas. B. P. Curtis	1888-1890
Oliver S. Smith	1888-1890
Hiram Johnson	1890-1892
Philip P. V. M. Botsford	1890-1892
Roger Sherman	1892-1894
Frank Westcott	1894-

MEMBERS OF CONSTITUTIONAL
CONVENTIONS.

Francis J. Prevost	1846.
Josiah Turner	1866-1867
S. Titus Parsons	1866-1867

PROBATE JUDGES.

Elias Comstock	1837-1840
Ira B. Howard	1840-1844
Amos Gould	1844-1848
Luke H. Parsons	1848-1852
Robert R. Tompson	1852-1856
John B. Barton	1856-1860
Hugh McCurdy	1860-1864
Sullivan B. Kelsey	1864-1880
Amasa A. Harper	1880-1888
Mathew Bush	1888-

COUNTY SURVEYORS.

Daniel Gould	1838-1840
Palander T. Maine	1840-1840
Nelson Ferry	1842-1846
Andrew Huggins	1846-1852
Josiah B. Parker	1852-1854
Andrew Huggins	1854-1856

POPULATION OF SHIAWASSEE COUNTY.

Cities.

Owosso.	1884.	1890.
1st Ward.........	2283	1836
2nd "	2008	1671
3rd "	1270	841
4th "	2708	2156
Totals.............	8274	6504

Corunna.		
1st Ward.........	875	785
2nd "	631	528
3rd "	265	278
Totals	1851	1382

Incorporated Villages.

Bancroft.............	640	648
Byron...............	428	413
Durand	901	255
Laingsburg..........	790	684
Morrice.............	421	420
Perry	336	420
Vernon	426	585
Totals...........	4161	3409

Townships.

Antrim	842	929
Bennington	1274	1298
Burns	1406	1167
Caledonia	1402	1387
Fairfield............	978	977
Hazleton............	1785	1801
Middlebury.........	91	965
New Haven	1620	1732
Owosso	1133	1161
Perry	1903	1906
Rush	1347	1302
Sciota..............	1387	1448
Shiawassee.........	1928	1592
Venice..............	2289	1414
Vernon	2477	2261
Woodhull...........	860	869
Totals.............	20,193	22,206
Grand totals......	32,537	30,958

County Officials.

1. Matthew Bush (Probate Judge).   2. Frank H. Watson (Prosecuting Att'y).
3. W. H. Bigelow (Register of Deeds).   4. Wm. E. Jacobs (Sheriff).   5. Duane C. Cooper (Clerk).
6. Rudolph Colby (Treasurer).   7. Geo. T. Mason (County Drain Com.).

BRIEF SKETCHES

—OF SOME OF—

Shiawassee County's Representative Citizens.

Alchin, Henry, was born in Kent county, England, June 29, 1832. He emigrated to America in the spring of 1850, in company with his parents, who settled in the township of Pittsfield, Washtenaw county, Mich.; afterward residing in the townships of Saline and York, same county, till 1860. March 4, 1860, he enlisted in Company "L" First Regiment U. S. Sharpshooters (Berdan's), being mustered into the —— at Detroit, shortly after joining his regiment at Hampton, Va. Following the fortunes of the army of the Potomac, through its many trials, successes, and reverses, from Yorktown to Petersburg, where, owing to the expiration of his term of service, he was discharged March 4, 1865, never having seen the inside of a hospital on his own account, and never having been wounded but twice, and then but slightly.

He was married Sept 24, 1865, to Miss Sarah A. Culver, of York township. The same year (1865) he settled in the township of Burns, Shiawassee county, on a new farm, clearing fifty acres in the short space of eight years. In March, 1873, he moved to his present residence, where he has improved as many more acres of wild land. January 10, 1895, his wife died, after a short illness. In the fall of 1885 he moved with his family to Virginia, locating near Malvern Hill, but not being successful, he moved back to his "old home" in Vernon township, Shiawassee county, in the spring of 1890. September 18, 1893, Mr. Alchin was again married to Miss Anna Jevne of Dundee, Monroe county, Mich. Mr. Alchin is one of the well-to-do farmers of Vernon township, and is highly respected by all his acquaintances.

Abrey, George T. & Co., Proprietors of the Woodlawn Park addition to Owosso. This piece of property is in the eastern part of the city and comprises a strip of land over half a mile wide, extending from the south line of the city north to the southerly bank of the Shiawassee River, and having over one mile frontage on the river. This land is entirely within the third ward of the city.

It is traversed by ten miles of streets, more of which are already graded. The street cars run through the center of it, and neat and comfortable houses have been built in almost every part; by the families who own and occupy them. Woodlawn Park, formerly known as the old Byerly farm, was noted for its beautiful fields and very productive soil. Here are located a part of the T. & A. A. car shops. The city water works and the city have purchased another nine-acre piece of land in this addition, on which is a large spring that furnishes abundance of pure water for the city. The owners of Woodlawn Park, George T. Abrey & Co., are selling lots at low prices and easy payments, and many are purchasing, believing that the property will advance rapidly.

Atherton, E. S., attorney at law at Durand, was born in Genesee county, Mich., Sept. 11, 1870. He was educated in the common schools of the county and at the Fenton Normal school, graduating from the teachers' department of the latter in July, 1890. In August of the same year he began the study of law, and was admitted to the bar in August, 1892, in Genesee county. He began the practice of his profession in Durand, October, 1892, and has succeeded in building up a good business. He is a member of several secret organizations, among which can be mentioned the A. O. U. W. and the F. & A. M., also the Modern Woodmen.

Bacon, George, the well-known merchant of Shaftsburg, Michigan, was born in Woodhull township, this county, in 1859. The early years of his life were spent on a farm, but he has been a resident of Shaftsburg since he was eighteen years old. He was married Nov. 18, 1861, to Miss Addie Vandwalker, who was also a native of Woodhull township. Mr. Bacon is one of the leading business men of Shaftsburg. Besides conducting a general store, where he carries a complete line of dry goods, boots and shoes, etc., he is also interested in the manufacture of lath. He belongs to one of the oldest families in the county, his parents having come here from the State of New York in 1849. He is well-known throughout the township, and enjoys a large and growing trade.

Barclay, Alexander, farmer of New Haven township, was born in Ayrshire, Scotland, June 11, 1830. Come to America in 1852, and first located in New York State. From there he moved to the State of Ohio, where he resided for two years, coming to Michigan in 1856. Mr. Barclay has been twice married, first on June 7, 1869, to Miss Helen E. Simmons; to that union was born three children, one of whom is now living. His wife dying in 1876, he was again married Jan. 28, 1879; his second wife, Hannah C. Curry, dying on July 18, 1890. One child was born to this union.

Becker, J. A., the leading merchant tailor of Corunna, is a native of Canada, having learned the tailors' trade there. He is a graduate of the Cleveland, Ohio cutting school for men's and ladies' fashions, and is a

first-class workman in every respect. He has been a resident of Corunna since 1895, and during that short time has succeeded in building up an extensive business.

Beahan, George F., a well-known merchant of Lennon, Mich., is a native of the State of New York, but has been a resident of this county for the past six years. In 1887 Mr. Beahan went west, and for some time was engaged in mining in Idaho, and farming in Dakota. On his return to Michigan he purchased a large elevator at Lennon, where he now purchases a large percentage of the grain crop of this county. He also handles a general line of seeds, and does an extensive business in grains of all kinds. Mr. Beahan is recognized as one of the progressive business men of Shiawassee county, and has by industry built up a large business in which he takes a just amount of pride.

Beatty, David, farmer of Hazleton township, was born in Mercer township, Butler county, Pa., Dec. 15, 1829. He was educated in the common schools of his native town, and continued to reside there until twenty-three years of age. Mr. Beatty came to Michigan in 1854, and first located at Corunna, where he followed the carpenter's trade for thirteen years. From there he moved to Hazleton township, and purchased a farm on section 12, where he now resides. He was married in marriage Jan. 20, 1859, to Miss Charity Vedder, a native of Oakland county. To this union have been born eight children, all of whom are living. Mr. Beatty is held in high esteem by the people of his township, and has served them as highway commissioner and school director.

Beatty, William Franklin, the subject of this mention, was the oldest son of David and Charity Beatty. He was born in Corunna, Michigan, Nov. 11, 1859. He lived with his parents in Corunna until 1876, when they removed to the township of Hazelton, where Mr. Beatty has since resided. During the winters of 1878, '79 and '81 he taught school, working on his father's farm during the intervening time. In the spring of 1882 he entered the employ of C. K. Runnells as clerk in a general store, remaining with him nearly two years, and with Vlem & Mackay, successors to C. K. Runnells, for about the same period of time. In May, 1885, he entered into a co-partnership with Washington Snyder, in a general store in New Lothrop, which business was successfully carried on until 1895, when they dissolved by mutual consent. Mr. Beatty retaining the business. Dec. 11, 1880, he married Miss Nellie V. Campbell of Imlay City, Mich., who was born at Fenton, Oct. 6, 1860.

Mr. and Mrs. Beatty are members of the Methodist Protestant Church of New Lothrop, and Mr. Beatty is a member of Farmer's Lodge No. 319, I. O. O. F. By industry and close attention to business, Mr. Beatty has established a large, growing trade.

Bement, Chas. H., present editor and proprietor of the Laingsburg News, of Laingsburg, Mich., was born at Ovid, Mich., March 4, 1871, and graduated from the high school of that place in 1888. Mr. Bement learned the printer's trade at Ovid, and followed it at different points throughout Shiawassee county until 1893, when he purchased the Laingsburg News. Since purchasing the above paper, he has increased his facilities for job work, and has enlarged the paper from a seven column folio, to a five column quarto. It is ably edited, and is bright and newsy throughout.

Benjanit, William O., proprietor of the Byron Marble Works, was born in Jefferson county, New York, where he remained until sixteen years of age. He served an apprenticeship of three years in the marble cutting trade, and has followed that as an occupation through life. Mr. Bennett has been in business in different towns in the State of Michigan, among which can be mentioned Carr, Ludington, Flint, and Owosso. It was from the last named place that Mr. Bennett came to Byron. He was married in 1875 on Christmas day to Miss Amelia Post, also a native of New York. To this union have been born seven children, two sons and two daughters living. Mr. Bennett is a superior workman in his line, and takes great pains to give his patrons superior goods. Judging from his past success, we doubt not but that he will build up a substantial trade, and remain one of Byron's citizens.

Benson Bros., the well-known furniture dealers and funeral directors of Laingsburg. This firm consists of Mr. J. H. and W. B. Benson. Both of these gentlemen are natives of Addison county, Vermont, Mr. J. H. having been born there in 1840, and Mr. W. B. in 1848. The early years of their lives were spent in farming, and they have been engaged in different lines of business throughout the country. Mr. J. H. Benson when twenty years old was appointed to a position in the U. S. Treasury, which he held for five years, and was then engaged in the mercantile business in Vermont. In 1874 he came to Laingsburg and established the business which they are now operating. Since becoming a resident of this place, he has filled a number of official positions, such as justice of the peace, city clerk, and a member of the school board. W. H. Benson, the junior member of the firm, is a thorough architect and builder. He came to Laingsburg in 1878, and since that time has been engaged more or less in contracting and building in this place. He has served the people as a member of the city council, and also on the board of education. This firm carries a complete line of furniture and funeral supplies. They have by careful attention to business built up a large trade, which extends throughout this and adjoining counties.

Bigelow, William H., the present registrar of deeds of Shiawassee county, was born in Oswego city, New York, July 27, 1852. Came with his parents to Ypsilanti, Michigan, when a child, and there grew to manhood, obtaining his education in the common and high schools of that place. In 1873 Mr. Bigelow removed to Saginaw, where he found employment as a clerk for five years. He then engaged in the drug business at Byron, Shiawassee county, which he conducted for five years. During that time he served both as village recorder and treasurer of Burns township. He afterward engaged in business at Owosso, in company with his brother, under the firm name of Bigelow & Bigelow, and continued in that business until his election as registrar of deeds, in the fall of 1888. Mr. Bigelow has four times been elected to this office and is now serving his fourth term. He was united in marriage April 23, 1874, to Miss Adelaide K. Brooks, daughter of Wm. Brooks of Lenawee county. To this union have been born two children, both of whom are now living. Mr. Bigelow is a member of the State Pharmaceutical Association and is a registered pharmacist. Socially, he is a member of the Knights of Pythias, and a Knight Templar in Corunna Commandery, and is also a member of other secret orders. In politics he is an ardent Republican, and is recognized as one of the leaders of that party in Shiawassee county.

Brown, Perry D., farmer of Venice township, was born in this State in the year 1846, and has been a resident of Venice township the greater part of his life. In 1875 Mr. Brown was united in marriage to Miss Lizzie J. Field. To this union were born three children, two sons and one daughter, all of whom are now living. He and family are pleasantly situated on a good farm of two hundred and sixty-two acres, which is under a high state of cultivation. He is considered one of the solid men of the township.

Bilhimer, A. M., farmer of Bennington township, was born in the State of Pennsylvania, Dec. 16, 1853, and came with his parents to the State of Michigan in 1864. Mr. Bilhimer was united in marriage Oct. 13, 1884, to Miss Minnie Henspeter. To this union has been born one child, a daughter, Florence. Mr. Bilhimer has followed farming as an occupation through life and has also been quite largely interested in stock breeding. In politics he is an ardent Republican and is recognized as one of the solid men of the township.

Bilhimer, F. B., farmer of Caledonia township, was born in Westmoreland, Pa., March 22, 1858. He came with his parents to Michigan when six years of age and located first in Owosso township, and resided there for twelve years. He then purchased a farm on section 31, Caledonia township, which he now owns and operates. He was married Jan. 4, 1882, to Miss Mary Leffingwell, a native of Wyoming county, New York. To this union has been born one child, a daughter. Mrs. Bilhimer's parents were originally from Vermont; her father coming to Michigan in 1865, and settling in Bennington township, where he resided until his death, Feb. 10, 1888.

Mr. Bilhimer has one of the best improved farms in the county, on which he has erected a fine home. He is well known throughout this township and has many warm friends. He was elected justice of the peace April 1, 1895, and also appointed health officer for that township.

Bilhimer, John F., a well-known farmer and fruit-raiser of Caledonia township, was born in Westmoreland county, Pa., April 6, 1849. The early years of his life were spent at his boyhood home, but in the spring of 1862 he came to Michigan, and settled in Shiawassee Co. He was united in marriage, Feb. 11, 1885, to Miss Florence Aken, who was born in Lorain Co., Ohio, June 9, 1864. To this union two children have been born, both of whom are living. Besides carrying on general farming, Mr. Bilhimer is extensively engaged in the growing of small fruits. They have a good farm, located on section 31, this township, which is under a high state of cultivation. He has served the people of his township as highway commissioner and school inspector. Mr. Bilhimer and wife are members of the Baptist Church, and are highly respected by the people of their township.

Black, Geo. R., & Son, the pioneer dry-goods firm of Owosso, and successor to the old firm of Geo. R. Black. Mr. Geo. R. Black, the founder of the business, was born at Clarence, Erie Co., N. Y., August 7, 1831, and it was there that he spent the early years of his life. He first began business as a clerk, and followed that profession for four years, when he moved to Nashville and opened a general store, which he conducted for one year. In 1856 he came to Owosso and started the business in which he is now engaged. Mr. Black was united in marriage, April 4, 1855, to Miss Mary H. Heath. Three children were born to them, one son and two daughters. The son, Mr. F. H. Black, was born in Owosso, and is now the junior member of this firm. He is one of the city's brightest young business men, and has assisted largely in the building up of their now large business. The daughters are now Mrs. C. E. Wheelock of Peoria, Ill., and Mrs. P. M. Roth of Owosso. Geo. R. Black and Son now occupy one of the finest stores in Central Michigan. Their stock is complete in every department, and by honesty and fair dealing they have built up the largest business in Owosso. Mr. Black, Sr. has filled many places of honor. He served the people eight years as a member of the city council, and has also served in other official capacities. He is a member of the Masonic Fraternity, and is well known in that order throughout the State.

Byerly, E. P., & G. W. Loring. These gentlemen have for the last thirty years been prominent residents and business men of Owosso. In 1889 the present partnership was formed, and for six years they have carried on a most creditable business in the real estate, loans, insurance, and pension business. Both served in the Union army, Mr. Loring in the 7th Ohio Infantry, while Mr. Byerly was in the 4th Michigan Cavalry; the latter was afterward honored as captain in the 10th Michigan Cavalry. He is now serving his second term as justice of the peace, an office which he conducts in a straightforward manner, characteristic of the man.

Black, B. D., the well-known druggist of Bancroft, was born in Wisner township, Tuscola Co., this State, May 28, 1866. He was educated in the common schools and followed school teaching for three years. Mr. Black began the study of pharmacy under Dr. Harvey, of Bancroft, and is now a regestered pharmacist. In 1889 he purchased a half interest in the drug business with Dr. Harvey, and later bought the entire stock. He not only carries a full line of drugs but also a very attractive stock of books and stationery. Mr.

Black was married in June 1888, to Miss Frances M. Gilligan, a native of Lapeer county, this State, to which event he attributes in a large degree the success he has met with, Mrs. Black being a thorough business woman.

He has served the people of Bancroft as recorder four years, and in June 1894 was appointed postmaster at that place. He has made many improvements in the office, and by courteous treatment of his patrons, has made it the best village post-office in the county. He is a success as a business man and enjoys a large trade.

Brand, James C. This gentleman is one of Durand's oldest citizens, and was the first man to platt any part of that village, which he did July 20, 1877. He was born at Brookfield, New York, August 30, 1821, and resided in that State for thirty-one years. In 1853 Mr. Brand came to Michigan and located in Ingham county, township of Phelps, section 20, where he purchased a farm which he traded for property in Lansing. He afterward resided in Clinton county five years, and it was in the latter place that he first began the manufacture of staves, which business he followed for eighteen years. At the end of that time, he came to Durand, which was then known as Vernon Center, and has resided there since that time. Mr. Brand was married Aug. 20, 1890, to Miss Maryette Kitchen, who came to this State from Ontario, Canada, in 1871.

Brewer, Emory L., the well-known boot and shoe merchant of Owosso, Michigan, is a native of Otsego county, New York. At the age of twelve years, his parents came to Shiawassee county and settled in Bennington township, and it was there that the early years of his life were spent. He was educated in the schools of this county, following this with a course in the Agricultural College, leaving there in the summer of 1859. At the breaking out of the war, he enlisted August 30, 1862, in Company K of the fifth Michigan Cavalry, and was discharged Oct. 13, 1864, with the rank of lieutenant. He was seriously wounded May 28, 1864, at Hawes Shop, Va., from which he has never fully recovered. January 1865, he began the study of law at Lansing, which he pursued for nearly two years, acting during that time as clerk of the supreme court. In 1868 he engaged in the boot and shoe business at Owosso, in company with his father-in-law, and of this business he is now the sole owner. In politics Mr. Brewer is an ardent Prohibitionist, and was nominated as lieutenant governor on that ticket in 1892. He has been a life-long worker in the cause of temperance, and is well known throughout this State.

Barnard, J. W., & Co., proprietors of the steam saw mill at Durand, Mich. This firm manufactures all kinds of hardwood lumber and boat oars. They do an extensive business in this line, and have one of the best equipped mills in this part of the State, their trade extending to all parts of the United States. Their business is one of the leading industries of Durand, and these gentlemen are recognized among her most substantial citizens.

Brown, Adam H., one of the pioneers of Shiawassee county, was born in the town of Niagara, Lincoln Co., Canada, Nov. 27, 1834.

Mr. Brown came to Michigan in 1870, and settled in Hazelton township on section 34, where he cleared and improved one hundred and twenty acres of land, and where he resided until the time of his death, July 14, 1894. He was united in marriage to Miss Mary M. Lewis, Nov. 15, 1860. To this union were born four children, Albert V., Sept. 8, 1862; Annie C., August 4, 1866; Dewey F., Feb. 2, 1874; and Ethel S., Feb. 8, 1882. The farm is now carried on by his two sons, Dewey F. and Albert V. Besides general farming, they are engaged in the breeding of Poland China swine, which they ship to all parts of the State. They have been unusually successful in this line of business, and are among the progressive men of the township.

Bumps, Frank F., a well-known attorney of Owosso, Michigan, was born at Bangor, Me., June 26, 1861, and came to northern Michigan with his parents when twelve years of age. He received his early education in the schools of Muskegon, and completed it by a course in the university of Michigan from which he graduated in 1887, with the degree of *Ph. B.* For some time after graduation, Mr. Bumps followed school teaching, and filled the positions of principal and superintendent in the public schools at different places, for five years. He began the study of law with Honorable S. S. Miner, of Owosso, and was admitted to the bar, May 23, 1892. He at once formed a partnership with Mr. Miner, which existed for one year; since that time he has practiced alone. Mr. Bumps has been twice elected circuit court commissioner and is now serving his second term. He has been more than ordinarily successful in the practice of his chosen profession, and enjoys a large and growing practice.

Bush, Judge Matthew, present judge of probate of Shiawassee county, was born at Marbletown, Ulster Co., N. Y., Dec. 6, 1853. His early life was spent on a farm, and later he began teaching district schools, which profession he followed for some time; this was for the purpose of obtaining sufficient means to pay his way while obtaining an academic education, and also while studying law. This he picked up, as it were, while working for Winter & Bros., at Rondout, New York, they having a line between their two stores. He afterward learned telegraphy and followed that for a short time. He began the study of law in August, 1873, and was admitted to the bar in September, 1876, at Saratoga, New York. He first began the practice at Kingston and remained there until 1879. In that year he came to Shiawassee county, and for a short time was in partnership with Alex. McKercher. He then practiced alone until the fall of 1888, when he was elected to the present office, the duties of which he has ably discharged. Judge Bush has been twice married, first to Miss Flora McKercher, who died in May, 1883. To this union was born one child, Walter, now thirteen years of age. He was again married in 1887, to Miss Annie Verney, a native of Calhoun county, Michigan. To this union have been born four children, three of whom are boys. Judge Bush is a member of the Masonic Fraternity, the I. O. O. F., and other secret orders. In politics he is an ardent Republican.

Byam, Edward O., a farmer of Vernon township, was born in the town of Guilford, Medina Co., Ohio, Jan. 6, 1841. Came with his parents to Michigan in 1850, and settled on the Indian reservation in Burns township. Mr. Byam was educated in the schools of this county, and has followed farming as an occupation through life. He was married Oct. 14, 1868, to Miss Mary Jane Prior, a native of England, who came with her parents to this country when three years of age. To this union have been born six children, four of whom are now living. Mr. Byam is one of the well-to-do farmers of Vernon township, and is the possessor of one hundred and eighty acres of good farm land on sections 30 and 31, which is under a high state of cultivation.

Castree & Shaw. This firm are well-known manufacturers of Owosso, and produce the Dedrick Patent Baling press, The Steel Star Land Roller, and are manufacturing Whipple Patent Adjustable Wagon-tire, also doing an extensive business as jobbers of engines, boilers, separators, saw-mills, etc.

Mr. J. B. Castree, the senior member of the firm, was born in Dudley, Worcestershire, Eng., Nov. 17, 1845. At an early age he learned the trade of a machinist, and followed it in his native land until 1869. In that year he came to America and located first at Flint, Mich., where he found employment in the general machine shops of that place.

Mr. Charles J. Shaw, the junior member of this firm, was born at Clarkston, Oakland county, this State, July 6, 1868. His parents removed to Flint, Mich., when he was two years of age, and it was there that his early life was spent. In 1880 he began learning the trade of a machinist, and has followed that profession since that time. In company with his present partner, Mr. Castree, he purchased the business of Castree, Mallery & Co., at Flint, which they operated for three years. In July, 1883, they removed their plant to Owosso, and are now located on South Shiawassee street, where they are doing a thriving business. Their hay presses and land rollers have only been on the market since last February, yet the success that they have met with has been far beyond their expectations.

Carland, M. & J., is one of the best known dry-goods firms in Shiawassee county. The senior member of the firm, Michael Carland, was born in Ireland, July 12, 1835. When scarcely a year old his parents came to America and settled in Oswego Co., N. Y., and from there they moved to Detroit in 1839. In 1865 the subject of this sketch came to Corunna and opened a retail grocery, which he conducted until 1884, when he enlarged the business by adding a complete line of dry-goods, boots, and shoes. The junior member of the firm, Mr. J. Carland, was born at Grass Lake, Mich. in 1850. He was educated in the Corunna schools, and in 1868 was taken in as a partner in this business. This firm is one of the oldest business houses in Shiawassee county, and does an extensive business, occupying two large store-rooms and employing a number of clerks. They not only handle a first-class line of goods, but pay the highest market price for all kinds of produce.

Carr, Edward, a well-known real estate and money-loaner of Corunna, Mich., was born in Sparta, Canada, Aug. 1, 1856. Since twelve years of age Mr. Carr has been dependent on his own resources. At the age of fifteen he learned the trade of a harness-maker and while following that as a journeyman, he came to Corunna in 1877. Three years later he embarked in the harness business for himself, and continued in that business until 1894. During that time Mr. Carr established three different places of business,—one at Owosso, one at Vernon, one at Corunna,—and under his management they proved a financial success. For the past few years Mr. Carr has been largely interested in the real estate and loan business, and now owns over three hundred acres of good improved land in this county besides a number of houses and lots. He was married March 7, 1881, to Frances A. Young, a resident of this county. Mr. Carr is what is known as a self-made man. He has by energy and close attention to business accumulated a respectable fortune, and by honesty and fair dealing has made many warm friends throughout the county.

Case, B. Warren, (Deceased), farmer of Shiawassee township, was born in Wayne County, N. Y., Oct. 18, 1830, and when a child moved with his parents to Indiana, residing there until 1851. In that year he visited Australia, where he followed mining, and also served in the police force for some time. He also visited Europe, Africa, and South America, spending over three years on this trip. In 1855 Mr. Case came to Michigan, and purchased a farm in Antrim township, this county, which he afterward disposed of and purchased the present home. He served in the great Rebellion, enlisting in the fall of 1861.

He was married May 4, 1865, to Lucy J. Daty, a resident of this county. To this union was born one son, Frank D., who since his father's death in February, 1892, has with his mother taken entire charge of their large farm. During his life Mr. Case was recognized as one of the enterprising and leading men of his township, which by his death lost one of its most respected and useful citizens.

Cooper, George A., farmer of Bennington township, was born Dec. 25, 1847, in this township. He was united in marriage, June 18, 1880, to Miss Harriett E. Betsias. To this union have been born two children, a son and a daughter. Mr. Cooper has followed farming as an occupation through life, and now owns a part of the farm on which he was born. He is a member of the Owosso lodge No. 81 of the F. and A. M., and the Owosso Chapter of the R. A. M. He is well known throughout the township, and has many friends and acquaintances.

Cooper, Duane C., the present county clerk of Shiawassee county, was born in Bennington township, this county, in 1845. He was educated in the common schools of the county and in the Corunna high school, and has followed farming and school-teaching the greater part of his life. During the late war Mr. Cooper served as a sailor on the iron-clad "Fort Hindman" under Admiral Porter on the Mississippi and Red rivers. At the close of the war he returned to his home in Shiawassee county, where he followed farming for a number of years. Mr. Cooper has served the people of Shiawassee county in numerous official capacities, serving seven years as supervisor of the township of Caledonia, and also seven years as township superintendent of schools, eight years as a member of the board of school examiners, and in other minor offices. As an official Mr. Cooper has given entire satisfaction to the people of the county. His straightforward manner, and his readiness ever to defend the cause of right and justice, have made him many warm friends throughout the county.

Collins, Joseph H., the present deputy county clerk of Shiawassee county, and also a member of the bar is a native of this county, having been born in Corunna, in 1873. He received his education in the schools of the county, graduating from the Corunna high school in 1891. He began the study of law with Mr. Seldon S. Miner in that year, and was admitted to the bar in June, 1894.

Mr. Collins was appointed deputy clerk by the present clerk, Mr. D. C. Cooper, and is now discharging the duties of that office. He is a young man of ability, and is well and favorably known throughout the county.

Collins, Will E. & Co., the pioneer drug house of Owosso. Mr. Will E. Collins, the junior member of this firm, is a native of Farmington, Oakland county, having been born there May 25, 1869. His father, Mr. J. W. Collins, enjoys the distinction of having been the first white child born in Farmington township, Oakland county. The subject of this sketch was educated in the common and high schools of this State and at the University of Michigan, from which he graduated in the pharmaceutical class of 1890. Soon after his graduation he secured a position in Bay City where he remained until 1893, when he came to Owosso and purchased his present business. Mr. Collins was united in marriage, Sept. 5, 1893, to Miss Berniece Osburn. The business conducted by Mr. Collins is one of the oldest in the city, and dates its existence from the early days of Owosso, when it was founded by Mr. J. F. Laubengayer. The store itself is one of the handsomest in the city, and has a well equipped laboratory in the rear.

Chapman, Odell, attorney at law, Owosso, Mich., was born in Caledonia township, this county, in 1859. He received his early education in the common schools, after which he entered the University of Michigan, graduating from the law department of that institution in 1880. Mr. Chapman was admitted to the bar in 1881, and began the practice of his profession in Owosso in the same year. In 1886 he formed a partnership with Mr. Frank Watson, and is now doing business under the firm name of Watson & Chapman. Mr. Chapman served the people as city attorney in 1888, and also in other official capacities. He is recognized as one of the leaders of the bar of Shiawassee county, and has been more than successful in the practice of his chosen profession.

Chase, M. L., the leading groceryman of Corunna, Mich., was born in Ontario county, N. Y., Jan. 3, 1857. He was educated at Clifton Springs Union School, and after leaving that school, followed farming for nine years. In 1886 Mr. Chase came to Michigan and entered the employ of Kelsey Brothers at Ionia, Mich., with whom he remained for one year. In 1888 he came to Corunna and purchased the store which he now occupies and where he carries a complete line of choice and fancy groceries. He was married July 8, 1878, to Miss S. Drake, of Newark, N. Y. Mr. and Mrs. Chase have many warm friends in Corunna, and he is considered one of the substantial business men of that place.

Chapell, W. R., real estate and insurance agent of Corunna, Mich., was born at Dexter, Washtenaw county, Mich., Sept. 25, 1848. Mr. Chapell has been a resident of Corunna for twenty-eight years, and was elected to the State legislature from this county in 1887 and 1888. He also served as postmaster at Corunna for eight years, and is at present a member of the Republican State Central Committee from the Eighth District, and chairman of the Republican County Committee of Shiawassee county. He is doing a large real estate and insurance business at Corunna, and enjoys an extended acquaintance throughout the State.

Chavannes, Fred A., farmer of Perry township, was born at Lausanne, Switzerland, Nov. 2, 1856. He came to America in 1876, and to Perry township in 1879, where he has since resided. Mr. Chavannes is one of the prosperous farmers of that township, and is well known and respected throughout the county.

Clark, W. H., president of the Shiawassee county Bank, was born in the State of Rhode Island, Oct. 26, 1825. He came with his parents to Michigan in 1832, and first settled in Oakland county. There he remained until 1830, working on a farm for nine dollars a month. In that year they moved to this county and settled in Shiawassee township on a farm which Mr. Clark now owns. He was engaged in the lumber business for nine years, and afterward in the grocery business, which he followed for three years. He was married April 10, 1851, to Miss Adelia Moore, a native of New York State. To this union have been born two children. Mr. Clark has been successful as a business man, and his advice is always sought on all questions of a public nature.

Clark, W. R., a well-know merchant of Laingsburg, was born in that place May 6, 1866. When twelve years of age he was thrown upon his own resources, and began life by selling the *Evening News*. Later he found employment as a clerk in the store of D. Lebar, with whom he remained for seven and one half years. Mr. Clark began business for himself in 1894, and now carries a general stock of Gents' Furnishing goods, groceries, boots, and shoes, etc. He was married in 1886 to Miss Carrie Honsberger. To this union have been born three children. Mr. Clark is now serving the people as town clerk and village assessor, and enjoys the respect of the people of that village and the surrounding country.

Corunna Coal Co., the, was organized in 1891, and is a successor to the old Corunna Coal Co. which began in 1872, and which was organized by H. B. Gilbert, George Tod, John Stambaugh, and George T. Perkins, George Tod being its president. This company existed until 1876. During the existence of this company Mr. Tod Kincade acted as secretary and treasurer and also as general manager. The first coal found in this county was discovered in the bed of the Shiawassee River, about two and a half miles from Corunna, in 1835. No mining, however, was done until about 1872, when the old Corunna Coal Co. was organized. The officers of the present company consist of the following named gentlemen: Tod Kincade, president, F. C. Gale, secretary and treasurer, J. C. Lovett, director. Mr. Kincade, its president, has had a wide experience in mining, and is now largely interested in gold mining at Cripple Creek, Col. The Corunna mine employs from eighty to a hundred men; it also owns machinery for mining. The coal is considered a superior steaming coal, and is consumed by manufactories and railroads.

Corunna Schools, the. The first school in Corunna was not a common public school, but a private enterprise taught by Uriah Dubois in 1840, in a log cabin. A district school was organized and taught in 1841 in the office of the registrar of deeds; but in 1843 Corunna erected a frame building on the site that has been devoted to the school ever since. Nelson Ferry was the first to guide the youthful minds within its walls. The one-story frame building which was then erected being inadequate to the growing demands of the village, a substantial brick structure was erected in 1851 on the same spacious grounds. Rev. S. P. Barker opened the school in the new building. He was followed by Mr. G. G. Doane, Mr. G. M. Reynolds, Mr. Wood, Mr. Haynes, and Mr. T. C. Garner, who did much to build up and increase the worth and reputation of our school at home and abroad in the ten years he was in our midst. Again did we find that we were growing not only mentally but so rapidly numerically that a cry for more commodious quarters must be heard. Hence, in 1866, a larger and more beautiful edifice was erected, and with the old, gives to our children a delightful place of learning. Our school has long had an enviable name, its instruction being sought by many foreign pupils. While the advanced studies have been taught and mastered, still it was given Mr. C. VanDorn to put our schools in line with the schools of the day by establishing a course of study, the first graduating class leaving our school in 1871. In that same year came to us as superintendent, Mr. H. C. Baggerly. He was a man of deep thought and untiring patience. His school was his life, and his life was a sublime lesson finished in our midst May 15, 1876. He was followed in 1876 by J. M. McGrath, a man of fine ability and much culture. The people of Corunna have always shown great interest in their school. They may well feel proud, for its diplomas entitled their holders to entrances without examination to the university and colleges of our State. It has a fine laboratory and apparatus necessary for the study of physics, and a choice library which will interest and attract pupils and aid them to understand "the true, the good, and the beautiful."

In 1881 the building and its contents were destroyed by fire, but out of the ashes speedily rose a building even more convenient and attractive. We had also as superintendents, Mr. Kingman, Mr. Farmer, Mr. Morse, Mr. McIntyre, Mr. Bumps, and Mr. Cupples. In 1890, at the suggestion of Prof. F. Bumps, and with his aid, an alumni society was formed which now claims one hundred members. In 1892 Mr. J. H. Monroe was called to the helm, a brainy man who permeates the whole school with the influence of his fine individuality. At present our school is under the supervision of Mr. Hudson Sheldon, who is one of its brightest alumni, being also an honored graduate of our own University of Michigan. Mr. Sheldon is a thorough student and an able thinker who is alive to the needs of the day. He is assisted by a corps of nine thoughtful teachers. Again we have a well equipped school building, an A No. 1 school. Corunna can well point with pride to her beautiful school building and grounds and the work her school is ever doing. The board of education consists of the following gentlemen: Irvin Evelth, Charles Holman, R. F. Kay, F. E. Welch, A. W. Green, A. L. Chandler, gentlemen who appreciate that the future demands her citizens to be educated morally, mentally, and physically.

Colby, Rudolph, present treasurer of Shiawassee county, was born in Shiawassee township, Sept. 12, 1853. He is the son of James S. and Eliza L. Colby, who came to this county in 1854. He was educated in the common schools of the county and at the Corunna High School. He has followed farming the greater part of his life, and is now the owner of one of the best farms in Shiawassee county. He has served the people in a number of public offices, being elected treasurer of Shiawassee township in 1885, and served as such for two years. He was then elected supervisor, and served for eight years in that capacity. In 1894 Mr. Colby was nominated by the Republican Convention of this county for the office of county treasurer, and was elected by an overwhelming majority. He was united in marriage Jan. 7, 1880, to Miss Georgiana Sergeant, who is also a native of this township. To this union have been born three children, two of whom are living. He is a member of the Masonic K. of P. and K. O. T. M. Fraternities and a director of the Bancroft Fair Association. He is well known, and has many warm friends throughout the county.

Colby, Walton L., the genial proprietor of the Colby House, of New Lothrop, was born in this county Jan. 11, 1862. The house which he is now operating was built by his father, and after his death, was purchased by our subject. He at once remodeled it and refurnished it throughout, and added to it a first-class livery and bus line. The house is now one of the best in this section of the country, and enjoys a large patronage. Mr. Colby was united in marriage Jan. 25, 1882, to Miss Ella Tozer. To this union have been born two children, both of whom are living.

Cox, Joseph C., farmer of Venice township, was born in Cuyahoga county, N. Y., June 23, 1815. He came to Michigan in 1830, and first settled in St. Clair county. He was married Feb. 9, 1840, to Miss Mary B. Carleton. To this union were born two children, John Z. and Eliza A. John Z. Cox was born in St. Clair county, July 13, 1841, and came to this county in 1882. He was united in marriage to Miss Angeline Granger, Jan. 2, 1881. Mr. Cox has lived on section 17 of this township for the last thirteen years, and has many warm acquaintances.

Corey, Marion D., proprietor of the City Steam Laundry at Owosso, was born in Ionia county, April 22, 1858. He received his education in the common schools of his native county, and completed it by a course in the Hillsdale College. At the age of eighteen he learned the carpenter's trade, which he followed for four years. He then entered the employ of his brother at Ionia, Mich., who was engaged in the laundry business at that place, and remained with him for two years. At the end of that time, in company with another brother, Frank W., he opened a laundry at Owosso and at Jackson under the firm name of Corey Brothers. This firm existed until February 1892, when his brother took the business at Jackson, Mr. Corey retaining that at Owosso. The City Steam Laundry is well equipped with the most modern machinery, and operates in connection with the laundry, a carpet-beating and renovating department. Mr. Corey has made many warm friends since coming to Owosso. He is an active member of the Maccabees, and the K. of P's., and he and wife are members of the Congregational Church.

Crum, J. D., M. D., one of Owosso's leading physicians, was born in Macoupin county, Ill., in 1855. He came to Michigan in 1875, and in the following year entered the Eclectic Medical Institute at Cincinnati, Ohio, graduating in 1881. Soon after his graduation, he came to Corunna, Mich., and there practiced for five years. In 1886 he came to Owosso, where he has since remained. Dr. Crum was married Dec. 31, 1878, to Miss Anna R. Cary, of Corunna. To them have been born four children, two sons and two daughters. Dr. Crum has also taken a special course of instruction in the Chicago Homeopathic Medical College, and at the Lincoln Park Sanitarium. He has been more than ordinarily successful in his practice, and to-day stands at the head of his profession in Owosso. The Doctor is a member of the Masonic Order, and also a Knight of the Maccabees, and has held official positions in both these orders.

Cudney, L. G., a well-known farmer of this county, is a native of Pennsylvania, having been born in the town of Girard, Nov. 21, 1855. He received his education in the academy at Springfield, Pa., and afterward taught bookkeeping and arithmetic in that institution. In 1874 he came to Michigan, and here learned the carpenter's trade, which he followed for a number of years. In 1879 he purchased a tract of timber land in this county which he has since cleared and improved until it is now one of the best cultivated farms in the county. He was married Dec. 21, 1881, to Miss Lenora Hoenshell, a native of Ohio. To this union have been born three children, a son and two daughters. Mr. Cudney is one of the best known farmers of Shiawassee county. He has by industry and close attention to business made for himself and family one of the most attractive homes in the county. He has many warm friends, and has often been urged by them to accept public office, but has always declined.

Crowe & Payne, dealers in agricultural implements, threshers, carriages, etc., at Owosso, Mich. This firm consists of Mr. W. Lee Crowe, and Mr. Will E. Payne. Mr. Crowe is a native of this county, having been born here Nov. 17, 1854. Mr. Payne was born in Isabelle county in 1863. Both of these gentlemen are thoroughly conversant with their business, having been engaged in it for a number of years past. This firm carries a complete line of agricultural implements, etc., threshers, carriages, surreys, wagons, harness, robes, blankets, and occupy the largest agricultural house in the State. They do a large business throughout this and adjoining counties, and are among the best known dealers in the State.

Countryman, H. F., merchant of Lennon, Mich., was born in the State of New York in the year 1869, and came to Swartz Creek, Mich., in 1876. Mr. Countryman was united in marriage to Miss Jennie McCracken in 1893. To this union has been born one child, a son,

June 21, 1894. Mr. Countryman has been engaged in general merchandise since 1892, at Lennon, where he carries a complete line of hardware and farming implements, etc. He has by careful attention to business built up a large trade, and enjoys the confidence of the people of his village and surrounding country.

Crandell, Enos W., chief engineer of the Owosso Manufacturing Co., was born at De Witt, Mich., March 4, 1854. Mr. Crandell's early life was spent on a farm, and he followed the occupation of a farm laborer until sixteen years of age, when he found employment in a saw-mill, and there took his first lessons in engineering. In 1884 he came to Owosso, and engaged with the firm of J. J. Parmalee as engineer and head sawyer. He soon resigned that position, however, to accept a similar one with D. Thompson & Co., now the Owosso Manufacturing Co., and remained with this company for eight years. He then accepted a position as traveling salesman with the Gratton Bridge and Manufacturing Co., and remained in the employ of that company until October, 1894, when he resigned in order to accept his old position with the Owosso Manufacturing Co.

Mr. Crandell was married July 4, 1877, to Miss Mary Dunker. To this union have been born three children, two sons and a daughter. He and wife are members of the M. E. Church, and he is the present president of the Stationary Engineer's Lodge No. 2 of Owosso, of which organization he is the deputy State organizer. Mr. Crandell is well known in Owosso, and at present represents the fourth ward in the city council.

Curry, Ira G., hardware dealer, of Owosso, Mich., was born at Fenton, Mich., June 2, 1863. He was educated in the public schools of Fenton, from which he graduated in June, 1881. He then completed his education by a course in the literary department in the University of Michigan, from which he graduated in 1886.

Mr. Curry has spent almost his entire life in the hardware business, having worked for his father in a general store and factory at Luther, Lake Co., Mich. On April 21, 1887, Mr. Curry came to Owosso, and purchased the hardware stock of Hopkins & Gould, which business he operated for one year. The following year he purchased another stock of hardware in the city and combined the two, this business he is now operating. Mr. Curry has taken an active interest in all matters pertaining to the city, and is now serving his second term as alderman. He is recognized as one of Owosso's most substantial business men, and by courteous treatment and fair dealing has built up a large and profitable business.

Dawes, Martin C., the present mayor of Owosso, was born at Cummington, Mass., June 10, 1832. He was educated in the academy of Holly, N. Y., and the common schools of his native State. In 1861 Mr. Dawes came to Michigan and engaged in the general mercantile business at Norville, Jackson Co., which he conducted until August, 1862, when he enlisted in Company F of the 20th Michigan Infantry, and served three years, being mustered out June 9, 1865, as captain of Company C. Mr. Dawes participated in many of the most important battles of the war, among which could be mentioned the Siege of Vicksburg, the Siege of Knoxville, Battle of the Wilderness, Cold Harbor, and many other minor engagements. At the close of the war he returned to Michigan and engaged in the foundry business at Manchester. In 1874 Mr. Dawes came to Owosso where he subsequently engaged in a wholesale oil, tobacco, and cigar trade, which he conducted until 1885. He then accepted a position as traveling salesman for a tobacco house, and traveled for over a year, then engaged in the wholesale cigar trade until March, 1892. He was married in 1853 to Miss Juliette Reed, of Holly, N. Y., who died Oct. 8, 1882. He later married Mrs. Emma F. Bristol, of Mason, Mich., in January 1884.

He has served as alderman for the second ward, and is now serving as mayor. He is also a member of the school board. Mr. Dawes is a member of the G. A. R., the Masonic Fraternity, and other secret orders. He is well known and highly respected in Owosso.

De Freun, Ferdinand, farmer of New Haven township, was born in Strasburg, Germany, June 10, 1850. In 1853 in company with his parents he came to Upper Canada, residing there for three years. They then came to Shiawassee county, Mich., where our subject has since resided. Mr. De Freun has a fine farm which he redeemed from the forest, and his success as a farmer fully proves the fact that farming pays. He is recognized as one of the leading men in the township.

Dickinson, C. S., farmer of New Haven township, was born at Wilmington, Windham Co., Vt., July 13, 1837, and continued to reside there until 1863, when he removed to New York City, residing there three years. From there he moved to Washington, D. C., and in the fall of 1865 came West. Mr. Dickinson came to Ann Arbor, Mich., in 1866, and followed railroading here for a short time, but in May, 1867, came to New Haven township and purchased eighty acres of land, which he now owns. He was married to Adelia Hotchkiss, July 16, 1866, who died May 11, 1881. Mr. Dickinson has served the people of his township as township treasurer for three years, and ably discharged the duties of the office of supervisor for seven years. He is now the owner of two hundred acres of good farm land, and is known as one of the most successful farmers of Shiawassee county.

Durrance and Burt, the well-known furniture dealers and funeral directors of Vernon. This firm consists of Mr. C. A. Durrance and Mr. Frank E. Burt. The junior member of the firm, Mr. Burt, was born in Lyons county, New York, Jan. 30, 1861, and came to Michigan in 1863, and to Vernon in 1866. He established their present line of business in 1881, which they have successfully carried on since that time. They carry a complete line of furniture and upholstering, also carpets and rugs, and do an extensive business throughout the county. They are recognized as one of the solid business firms of that place.

Duff, Charles C. This gentleman is one of Owosso's best-known business men. He is a native of this State, having been born in the town of Brest, Monroe Co., Dec. 16, 1842. Mr. Duff received a common-school education, and after the death of his father in 1848, moved to Lewis county, N. Y., where he engaged in farming and school teaching, and also worked for some time in a box factory. At the breaking out of the war, he was the first man to enlist in Harrisburg, N. Y., which he did April 28, 1861, as a member of Company B of the 35th N. Y. Volunteers, and was discharged with this regiment May 7, 1863. He however re-enlisted the same day with the 20th New York cavalry, and served with that regiment until August 31, 1865.

After the long marches of Pope's retreat, which commenced at Fredericksburg and ended at Antietam, during which time his regiment was engaged in the battle of Cedar Mountain, Georgetown, second Bull Run, Chantilla, South Mountain, and Antietam, his present disability, which began in the form of rheumatism some months before, had assumed such serious proportions that he was taken with the sick and wounded to the Patent Office hospital at Washington, where he remained five weeks, and returned to his regiment. Afterward, he was transferred to the Band of the regiment on account of his disabled condition.

His regiment was the first white troop to enter Richmond on the morning of April 3, 1865, and their band was the first to play the "Star Spangled Banner" and other national music in Richmond after its capture. At the close of the war he returned to Lewis county, N. Y., and shortly afterward came to Owosso and accepted a position as clerk in the grocery store of his brother-in-law, Mr. M. L. Stewart, and remained in his employ until 1870, when he engaged in the business for himself, and which he has successfully operated since that time.

In 1899 Mr. Duff erected the store building on Exchange street which he now occupies and where he conducts both a wholesale and retail grocery business.

He was married in 1866 to Miss Flora G. Graham, daughter of Dr. J. M. Graham. To this union have been born two daughters. During his long residence in Owosso, Mr. Duff has made many warm friends, and has built up a large and profitable business. Though a Republican in politics, he has never sought public office, but has often been solicited by his friends to do so.

Durham, William, a well-known farmer of Caledonia township, is a native of England, having been born in Somersetshire, Nov. 5, 1839. In 1850 he came to America and settled in Venice township, this county, where he resided with his parents until twenty-one years of age. At that time he purchased an eighty-acre farm in Caledonia township, which he afterward sold. He then purchased another farm in the same township, which he has added to from time to time, until he now owns one of the best improved farms in the county. Mr. Durham was married Sept. 15, 1867, to Miss Sutton, a native of Steuben county, N. Y. To this union have been born four children, two of whom are now living. Mr. Durham has been more than successful as a farmer, and now owns one of the most valuable farms of the county, the greater part of which is underlaid with coal.

Edgar, William, farmer of New Haven township, was born at Ayrshire, Scotland, May 30, 1845. When nine years of age he emigrated to America in company with his parents and first located in Sandusky county, Ohio, where they remained for two years. From there they came to Shiawassee county, Mich., where our subject has since resided. Mr. Edgar was married Dec. 18, 1879, to Miss Una Collins. To this union have been born four children. Mr. Edgar is well known in New Haven township and the farm which he now owns has been cleared almost entirely by himself. They have a pleasant home and are among the well-to-do people of that township.

Earle, Oscar, liveryman at Corunna, Mich., was born in the State of Ohio, Aug. 11, 1853. Came with his parents to Michigan when ten years of age and settled

in Berlin, Ionia Co. It was there that he received his education and continued to reside until 1887. In that year he came to Corunna and opened a livery and sale stable which he has successfully operated since that time.

Ely, William, the leading furniture dealer and undertaker of Corunna, was born in Jefferson county, New York, Feb., 3, 1830. When eleven years of age, his parents moved to Canada, where our subject learned the trade of a cabinet maker, which he has followed the greater part of his life. For three years he was engaged in selling watches, jewelry, etc., through different States. Mr. Ely was united in marriage on May 1, 1843, to Miss Mary Ann Newell. To this union have been born four children, all of whom are now living. Mrs Ely departed this life in the fall of 1890. Their son, Mr. N. W. Ely, at the age of seventeen years, occupied the responsible position of cashier for the F. & P. M. R. R., which he resigned in order to accept a position with Morley Bros., of Saginaw, wholesale hardware dealers of that city, and with whom he still remains. Their daughter, Nettie A., is now the wife of M. N. Simmons, who is general superintendent of Parmalee's bus line in Chicago. Mr. Ely is now doing an extensive business at Corunna and enjoys the largest trade in that city; and is second to none in the county. He is considered one of the substantial business men and enjoys the confidence and respect of the entire people.

Estey Manufacturing Co., the. This company is the largest of Owosso's industries, and to give a detailed account of its growth from year to year cannot be given in this limited space. It was first organized in 1878, and started operation in the building now occupied by the Estey Carriage Co., which was then located on the site of the present factory A, warehouse. In 1880 the present factory A was built. Three years following, what is known as warehouse No. 2, located parallel with the D. & M. R. R. tracks, was erected. In 1890 the large building, warehouse and factory, in which the offices are now located was erected, and which now gives a factory front on Washington street of four hundred and fifty feet and over two hundred feet on the D. G. H. & M. R. R. tracks. In 1891 the plant known as factory B, which is two hundred and fifty-six by eighty feet, was erected. This factory is devoted to the manufacture of a cheap and medium grade of goods, while in factory A, nothing but a superior grade of goods is made.

This company have also one of the finest band sawmills in the State, which is fully equipped with the latest machinery. They employ about five hundred men, and do a business amounting from seven to nine hundred thousand dollars per year.

The Estey Manufacturing Co. manufacture all kinds and grades of furniture, which find a market in all parts of the world. To this company is due the credit of having made Owosso the thriving city that it is to-day.

Evans, Alvin, one of Owosso's best-known citizens, was born in the State of New York, June 6, 1831. He came with his parents to Michigan when seven years of age and first located in Lenawee county, near the city of Adrian. Mr. Evans began business for himself when eighteen years of age, and first located in Muskegon; he afterward followed lumbering and merchandizing at Big Rapids for about thirteen years. He then came to Shiawassee county, and since that time has been engaged in estimating timber lands and making descriptions and maps of government lands for large lumber dealers throughout the State. He was united in marriage Dec. 18, 1862, to Miss Sarah A. Wallace, who was born in Sutesman county, N. Y., Oct. 11, 1844. To this union have been born four children; Geo. T., April 8, 1864, died Jan. 26, 1871; Wallace A., March 10, 1877, and died March 3, 1880; Albert B., Oct. 9, 1879; Vermer A., June 9, 1887. Mr. and Mrs. Evans are active members of the Baptist Church and are highly respected by the people of Owosso.

Evening Argus, The. This is the only daily paper published in Shiawassee county, and was founded July 21, 1892, by Messrs. J. N. Klock and R. C. Kinley. It is an eight-page, six-column paper, and is published both daily and weekly. It has done a flourishing business, and has a circulation of over twelve hundred in both departments. In politics it is independent. This paper was recently sold to Mr. George T. Campbell, former secretary of the Y. M. C. A. of this place. Mr. Campbell was formerly a newspaper man, and no doubt will keep *The Argus* up to its present high standard.

Exchange Bank, the, of Byron, Mich. This bank was organized in March, 1890. Its officers consist of the following gentlemen: Andrew Kohrabacher, president; William H. Hunt, vice-president; A. E. Hunt, cashier. This firm does a general banking business and enjoys a reputation of being one of the sound and reliable banks of Michigan.

Fauble, Cyrus, one of Durand's enterprising citizens, was born in Green township, Wayne county, Ohio, and was educated in the schools of that county. He came to Michigan in 1869, and located in Saginaw county, where he learned the carpenter trade and followed it for twelve years. He afterward purchased a sawmill at Redfield, Ohio, and has owned and operated twelve different mills. In July, 1894, Mr. Fauble came to Durand and purchased the land which is now known as Fauble's addition to that village. These lots are centrally located and are rapidly growing in favor, and a number of the best dwellings in the place have been erected there in the past year. Mr. Fauble was married on June 16, 1861, to Miss Catherine Franks, who was born in Hancock county, Ohio. To this union have been born five children, all of whom are now living. Mr. and Mrs. Fauble are both Seventh-day Adventists, and are well known and highly respected throughout the township.

Fitch, J. M., Secretary of the Durand Land Co. The village of Durand is situated sixty-seven miles northwest of Detroit, and is the junction of the D. G. H. & M. R. R., the G. T. R. R., the T. A. A. & N. M. R. R., and the terminus of the C. S. & M. R. R., giving railroad facilities from and to seven different points of the compass. For manufacturing purposes the location cannot be excelled in the interior of Michigan. In 1889 a company known as the Durand Land Co. was organized under the State law, and purchased several tracts of land, which was platted. A large portion of Durand has since that time been built up. Saginaw street, which is the main business street of the village, has several fine brick blocks, all of which have been erected since 1889. The growth of the town has surprised every one, and the recent action of the T. A. A. & N. M. R. R., in purchasing about twenty acres of land, the erecting of a round house, and in making Durand the central division of the road, has given to us what might be denominated a boom. The sound of the hammer can be heard in all directions early and late, and new houses are being erected as fast as nails can be driven and plaster spread. Every day,

property is changing hands. The Durand Land Co. have just opened up for sale the third and fourth additions, and have made a sub-division of out lots A., which is in the eastern part of the town, where lots can be purchased at reasonable figures for cash or on time with small payments down. There is an energetic lot of business men and women in Durand, who are at all times ready to meet competition and give as good a return for money received as any town in the State. Durand has three churches—Methodist, Baptist, and Holiness; also the Salvation Army barracks, and a fine high school building. In point of moral force and the observance of law Durand stands as well as our sister villages. The *Durand Express*, a live newspaper, which means a live editor, dispenses the local and general news once a week. The present directors of the Durand Land Co. are as follows: Edward Brown, president; Oliver B. Campbell, vice-president; J. W. Fitzgerald, treasurer; John M. Fitch, secretary; O. W. Munger, Porter K. Perrin, Geo. F. Mervin, Chas. E. Cook, Edward C. Cummins, Chas. C. De Camp.

French, J. Irving, proprietor of the flouring mills of New Lothrop, was born at Flushing, Genesee Co., Mich., Jan. 20, 1860. Mr. French first learned the milling business in Minnesota, and followed it there for some time, and afterward at Flushing, this State. April 1, 1895, he leased the New Lothrop mills, which are among the best known in the county. He was united in marriage March, 25, 1884, to Miss Myrtie Kimmell, a native of this State. To this union have been born five children, all of whom are living. Mr. French is a thorough miller and is conversant with the business in all its departments, and the flour produced at his mill is not excelled by any in the county.

First National Bank of Ovid. This bank was organized Nov. 20, 1884, with a capital stock of fifty thousand dollars and has at present a surplus of over ten thousand dollars. Its officers consist of the following gentlemen: H. A. Potter, president; W. R. Shaw, vice-president; and H. N. Keys, cashier. Its board of directors consists of the above named gentlemen, together with the following: N. J. Clark, J. E. Gerow, O. B. Campbell, H. P. Harris, and George A. Steel. The management of the bank is chiefly in the hands of Mr. H. N. Keys, who was born at Holley, N. Y., in 1858. He came to St. Johns, Michigan, in 1876, and to Ovid in 1882. Mr. Keys began the banking business in January, 1879, and by energy and close attention to business has made the Ovid bank one of the strongest in the State.

First National Bank of Corunna, the oldest bank and the *only* national bank in Shiawassee county. This well-known banking house was organized in 1865 by Judge Mc Curdy. Its first charter expired in 1885 and was then extended until 1905. The first officers of this bank were Hugh Mc Curdy, president and S. B. Reynolds, cashier. Mr. Reynolds filled that position until his death in 1871, after which Mr. A. T. Nichols was elected cashier, Mr. Nichols discharging the duties of that office until his death, June 17, 1894. On June 30, of that year, Mr. W. A. Ronakranz was elected to that position and is holding it at the present time. The present officers of this bank are the following well-known gentlemen: W. D. Garrison, president; L. W. Simmons, vice-president; W. A. Ronakranz, cashier; and W. T. Gallager, assistant cashier. Its board of directors comprises some of the wealthiest men of the county. It does a large business and is recognized as one of the solid banking houses of the State.

Frienske, J. & H., manufacturers and dealers in all kinds of building brick and drain tile, Owosso, Mich. Mr. Julius Frienske, the senior member of this firm, was born near Brandenburg, Germany, Feb. 10, 1842. His brother Herman, the junior member, is also a native of that place, being born there Dec. 17, 1844. They were both educated in the schools of their native land, and in 1863 in company with their parents emigrated to America, coming direct to Owosso, where they have since resided. In February, 1864, they enlisted in the 13th battery of Michigan light artillery and served with that battery until July 11, 1865, when they returned to Owosso and purchased a brick yard of Mr. Stattuck, which was the foundation of their present business. This business they have enlarged from time to time, until it is to-day one of the most extensive in that line in this part of the State. Both of these gentlemen are now members of the city council, Mr. Julius Frienske having served thirteen years, and Mr. Herman four years. The former served as mayor for the city for the year 1889, and the latter is now serving a sixth year as a member of the board of education. He also builds the responsible position of treasurer of the Shiawassee Saving Society. Both are members of the G. A. R., and Mr. Herman Frienske is now filling the position of senior vice-department commander of that order in the State.

Fuller, Alonzo C., the present supervisor of Sciota township, was born in Ingham county, this State, in 1848. He resided in that county for thirty-eight years, coming to Sciota township, this county, in 1893. Mr. Fuller was united in marriage to Miss Lucy Larabee, March 15, 1876. To this union were born four children, two sons and two daughters. Mr. Fuller, since coming to this county, has served the people three years as supervisor, and has so discharged the duties of that office as to give entire satisfaction to the people of this township.

Garfield, O. A., the well-known music dealer of Durand, was born in Oakland county, Mich., Sept. 18, 1853. He was engaged as traveling salesman the greater part of his life, for in a recent engaged in the sale of pianos, organs, and sewing machines. He carries a complete line of the above-named goods, and represents some of the largest manufacturers in the country. He does an extensive business and handles none but first-class goods. Mr. Garfield has served the people of Durand in a number of official capacities, and is now filling the office of justice of the peace.

Garrison, W. D. and A. G., proprietors of the Vernon Roller Mills. This firm is one of the oldest and most substantial business firms in Shiawassee county. They began business at Vernon, March 1, 1859. Besides operating the Vernon roller mills and elevator, they also do a general banking business. W. D. Garrison, the senior member of this firm, was born in the State of New York, in 1833, and came with his parents to Michigan in 1836. Mr. A. G. Garrison, the junior member, is a native of Oakland county, this State, having been born in that county in 1840, and came with his parents to Vernon in the fall of the following year. Mr. W. D. Garrison, besides being interested in the business referred to at Vernon, is also extensively interested in the First National Bank of Corunna, of which he is president.

Gould, Lineus E., attorney at law, of Owosso, is a native of this county (Shiawassee), having been born in Antrim township, Sept. 8, 1847. He is a son of Col. Eb. Gould, a sketch of whom appears elsewhere in this work. Our subject was educated in the schools of Owosso and at the Olivet College. He began the study of law with his uncle, the late Judge Gould of Owosso, and later entered the law department of the State University, graduating from there in 1871. He was admitted to the bar the same year of his graduation, and at once began practice in company with Judge Gould. In 1873 he was appointed attorney for the First national bank of Owosso, and filled that position for some time. In 1875 he was elected circuit court commissioner and filled that position continuously for eight years. In about 1886 Mr. Gould purchased the *Owosso Herald* which he operated for one year, then moved it to Owosso, and it is now known as the *Owosso Press*. He was again elected circuit court commissioner in 1886 and held it for two terms. Mr. Gould has not practiced for some years, but he is well and favorably known throughout this and adjoining counties.

Gould, Col. Ebenezer (Deceased). The subject of this mention was born in Fleming, Cayuga county, N. Y., April 16, 1811. He received a limited education in the common schools of his native State, and the early part of his life was spent on a farm and clerking in a store for his brother. In 1853, he came to Michigan and clerked at Auburn, Oakland county, where he afterwards engaged in business for himself. In the fall of 1857 he moved his stock of goods to Owosso, and resided in this city until the time of his death, Sept. 7, 1877. Col. Gould retired from the mercantile business in 1849, and for a short time afterward was interested in a grist mill at Owosso; this he later disposed of and engaged in farming in Antrim township. In 1860 he began the study of law with his brother, Amos Gould at Owosso, and was admitted to practice in the fall of 1853. He at once formed a partnership with his brother which existed until January, 1861. In July, 1861, he was offered the position of first major of the 8th Michigan Cavalry, which position he accepted, and was mustered into service in August of the same year. During the early part of his service this regiment was detailed on picket duty near Washington, and it was not until the battle of Gettysburg that they saw much active service. After the battle of Junktown, Maryland, Col. Gould was given command of the regiment and served in such until the battle of Hagerstown, where he was severely wounded and compelled to retire for a time from active service. He again joined his regiment in May, 1864, and was in active command during the battle of the Wilderness. He was compelled however to resign his position on account of disability and was honorably discharged Nov. 30, 1864, with the rank of colonel. At the close of the war he returned to Owosso and resumed the practice of law, being associated with Mr. G. R. Lyon for a number of years. We regret very much that limited space will not allow us to give a detailed history of Col. Gould's military and professional career. Suffice to say that both as a soldier and as a citizen he was ever ready to discharge any duty that fell to his lot. Col. Gould was married Dec. 2, 1845, to Miss Irene Beach. Daughter of Lucina Beach, of this county.

Gould, Amos. Few men in a generation are capable of so great and abiding industry and of such force and profusion of thought and of action as was Amos Gould. His life work, with its struggles, not must came, therefore have, was of such importance, and with his intelligence and upright course, was many times of his tempering influence of circumstances, but takes their position to influence and in the careers of plain reform. Amos Gould was born in Fleming in the neighborhood of Auburn, New York, Dec. 3, 1808. The force, vigorous and progressive characteristics of the English, united in his memory take the quiet, prudent, and steady qualities of the Hollander. His grandfather, Ebenezer Gould, received good service as a captain of infantry in the Revolution. His father's name was also Ebenezer, and his mother's maiden name was Polly Simmons. The father received a farm near Auburn in Cayuga county, and there Amos was born. His early advantages were both of education were those of a too-late life,—a little schooling in the winter, and a few books of the neighbors; and of his father's rich farm, well stocked, gave him more benefit than the ravenous reading of a large library would have given, and a desire for more education, for which he soon had opportunity to achieve. He afterward attended the academy at Auburn, Cayuga Co., and later entered Hamilton College, of Clinton, New York.

Mr. Gould had the great good fortune at the outset of his legal education to enter as a law student the office of Wm. H. Seward, the great Wm. Seward; a man possessed of comprehensive legal knowledge, powerful ability, and also of robust intellectual culture. After his legal career as a clerk for some time under Theodore Spencer, and of Chief Justice Spencer, he was admitted to the bar. Having opened an office, he met in Owosso the leading talent of the State, and the George Emerson was partner enjoyed a large practice. He was appointed by Hon. H. Seward, then governor, master of chancery, and by Chancellor Walworth, injunction master of the seventh judicial circuit. Owing to his health, and the duties of his brother and business career, for which he was known, he dissolved his partnership, surrendered a large amount of property, and moved to Owosso, Michigan, in 1843.

In the two-forty years of his life his services to the public identified him with every enterprise, not only on behalf of Owosso, which through his efforts largely, marches as Indian village to a prosperous city, but also in the larger and the enduring development of the State. Sound judgment, and a flexible, decisive statement of his case, and extensive information to his client's cause, made him one of the foremost lawyers in the State. In chancery, he was particularly strong, and it has been said by a prominent lawyer that he was in practice a greater value a jury in his brief ever listened to, and as master of habits slavery in chancery, has by a short, despair covenant of fact.

Since the second enactment of Mr. Lincoln, Mr. Gould's opinion inclined toward the Republican party, but his views of slight principles were more measured by law's ideal. As spectators for Owosso township from 1851 to 1856, as prosecuting attorney, as justice in the fall of 1849, as State senator in 1864; in all these he was a power, not that he was partisan, but a man of thorough and faithful in small, and as a State senator in 1859, he was impartial, and faithful to his constituents.

Garner, Robert, farmer of Hazleton township, was born near St. Mary's, Middlesex county, Canada, Sept. 4, 1851. Came to Hazleton township when seventeen years of age and has resided here since that time. He is the son of George and Ann Garner. His father was

born near St. Catherines, Canada, Nov. 12, 1818, and died in Hazleton township, this county, in 1883. His mother was born in England, May 14, 1821. They were married June 19, 1842, and were the parents of thirteen children. His mother is still living. Our subject was married to Miss Addie Jones of this township. To this union have been born three children, Fred, born Oct. 4, 1873; Nina, June 29, 1878; Trifreddo, Jan. 10, 1881. The parents of Mrs. Garner were R. and Rebecca Jones. Her father was born in New York, June 12, 1822, and died in this township, Oct. 13, 1873. Her mother was born in Ohio, Sept. 15, 1826, and is still living. They were married Dec. 5, 1849, and were the parents of ten children, four of whom are now living. Mr. Garner carries on general farming, and also follows the trade of a brick and stone mason. He has served the people of his township as drain commissioner, and is highly respected by all who know him.

Gilmore, William, a well-known farmer of Shiawassee county was born in Cavan county, Ireland, in 1831. He remained in his native land until nineteen years of age, when he emigrated to America and first located at Auburn N. Y., where he remained until 1853; he then moved to Wayne county, Michigan. In 1857 Mr. Gilmore came to Shiawassee county and purchased the farm on which he now resides near Gaines township. He was married in 1862 to Ann J. Stringer. To this union have been born nine children six of whom are still living. He and wife are members of the R. E. Church of Gaines. In politics he is a Prohibitionist. Mr. Gilmore has by industry made for himself and family one of the pleasantest homes in this township.

Gallagher, Willie, our subject is a native of New Haven township, having been born in this township June 15, 1881. Since six years of age he has made his home with Mr. Thos. Dowling, one of the well-to-do farmers of that township. Willie began school when six years of age and is a pupil in district 8 o, and has attended that school continuously since that time. He is a bright student and is now in the eighth grade, among the studies can be mentioned civil government, physiology, geography, and all other branches taught in the common school. The above plate is a good likeness of Master Willie and which he secured as a prize offered by the Atlas Publishing Co, for the best specimen of map drawing made by any pupil in the common schools of the county.

Goodspeed, Charles H., farmer of Shiawassee township, was born in Oswego county, N. Y., Feb. 22, 1834. He was educated in the common schools of that State and in 1849 came to Michigan and first located in Livingstone county. Mr. Goodspeed came to this county in 1859, and entered a quarter section of land on section 26 of Shiawassee township. He afterward disposed of this property, and in 1865 purchased fifty acres in the same township, on which he now resides. He was married March 28, 1858, to Miss Helen L. Adams, also a native of New York State. Four children have been born to them, three of whom are now living. Mr. Goodspeed is a member of the Masonic fraternity, and served the people two years as township treasurer, the duties of which office he discharged in a manner to refine as best credit upon himself.

Goodell, James M., attorney at law of Corunna, Michigan, is a native of New York, having been born at Le Roy, Genesee county, N. Y., Oct. 7, 1841. He came with his parents to Michigan at the age of thirteen and received his education in the schools of this State. He began the study of law with the Honorable Hugh McCurdy in July 1861 and was admitted to the bar in Sept. 1863. He at once began the practice of law at Corunna and has followed it there continuously since that time. Mr. Goodell was elected prosecuting attorney in 1864 and in 1866, and served as such for four years. He was elected circuit court commissioner in 1866, and also served as State senator in 1873 and '74.

Members of the Shiawassee County Bar.

Mr. Goodell has also filled a number of minor offices such as supervisor and mayor of the city. He enjoys a large practice and is recognized as one of the ablest attorneys in the county.

Godfrey, Charles E., embalmer and funeral director of Bancroft, Michigan, was born at State Line, Chautauqua county, N. Y., March 5, 1860. Our subject received his early education in the schools of his native State, and at the age of fourteen moved with his parents to North East Erie county, Pa., where he also attended the high schools and found employment in the organ and piano factory during the summer vacation. Learning the carvers' trade March 15, 1879, he came to Michigan and found employment at Owosso with the Estey Manufacturing company; later he entered the employ of Woodard Brothers' furniture works, and filled the position of foreman carver and designer for nearly four years. March 5, 1885, Mr. Godfrey embarked in business for himself at Bancroft, Mich., under the firm name of Murphy & Godfrey, which did a general furniture and undertaking business. In April, 1886, Mr. Godfrey purchased his partner's interest in the business, and since that time has operated it alone. Mr. Godfrey is a member of the Funeral Directors' Association of Michigan, and is well known throughout the State. In 1888 he erected a brick block twenty-five by a hundred feet in Bancroft, which he now occupies. He is also quite largely interested in real estate, and owns a farm of two hundred and forty acres near the village of Bancroft. He was married Aug. 20, 1891, to Addie E. Olney. To this union have been born two children, a son and a daughter, both of whom are now living. He has been a member of the village council, and is also a member of several secret organizations, among which can be noted, Bancroft F. & A. M. No. 382, Corunna Command, No. 21 K. T., and the I. O. O. F. lodge at Bancroft. Filling the highest offices in several of these bodies. In politics, he is a Republican.

Gute, George, this gentleman is well known to the people of Corunna and surrounding country. He is a

native of this State, having been born at Ann Arbor. When quite young, his parents moved to Owosso, and it was there that he received his early education and completed it by a course in the German and English schools of Detroit. After leaving school, Mr. Gute learned the brewers' trade, and followed it in Owosso until 1886. In that year he engaged in business which he followed for some time. Mr. Gute is now engaged in business at Corunna, and handles a full line of choice liquors, imported and domestic cigars.

Gulick, Henry J., farmer and blacksmith of Burns township, is a native of this county, having been born in Burns township on the farm now owned and operated by his father, Jacob Gulick. His education was obtained in the district schools, and at the age of twenty he began learning the blacksmith trade. In 1876 he engaged in business for himself and has followed it ever since. He is also interested in farming and stock raising, and has paid particular attention to the breeding of the thorough bred Poland China swine and Plymouth Rock chickens. He was married in 1878 to Miss Lizzie Tyler also of this township. Four children have been born to this union, all of whom are living. He and wife are members of the M. E. church, and he is well and favorably known throughout the township.

Glover, Mr. Francis, farmer of Middlebury township, was born in Canada, June 4, 1825. Mr. Glover was united in marriage, Nov. 20, 1855, to Miss Eliza Whitaker. Shortly after his marriage, he moved a few miles west of London, Canada, and in April 1865, came to Grand Rapids, Mich., where he remained for a few months, removing from there to southern Illinois. From there they moved to Shiawassee county, Mich., where they have since resided. Mr. Glover is one of the well-to-do-farmers of Middlebury township, and his farm is one of the best in the county.

Harding, Rev. Merritt S., farmer of Venice township, was born in Steuben county, N. Y., June 5, 1844. He removed from there to the State of Pennsylvania, where he resided for ten years, and then came to Michigan, where he has since remained. In 1883 Mr. Harding was united in marriage to Mrs. Ursilla Swinderman, who had three children by her first husband. To this union have been born five children, one of which is dead. During the late war Mr. Harding served as a member of Company H, 23rd Michigan Infantry, enlisting Sept. 12, 1862, and serving for three years and two months. He became disabled while in service, and has been unable to perform any manual labor since that time. He is well known throughout the township, and highly respected by all.

Hathon, Milson, farmer of Venice township, was born in Addison county, Vermont, in 1830. He came with his parents to the State of Michigan when three years of age, and has been a resident of this State since that time. Mr. Hathon was united in marriage in 1874 to Miss Jennie Lewis, a resident of Hazelton township, this county. To this union have been born seven children, all of whom are now living. Mr. Hathon is one of the progressive farmers of Venice township, and owns a fine farm of eighty acres, which is under a high state of cultivation.

Haber, Godfrey, farmer of New Haven township, was born in Wurtemburg, Germany, Aug. 5, 1844. He came with his parents to the United States when three years of age, and resided in different parts of this State for a number of years. When he was about thirteen years of age, he came to Shiawassee county, and settled on a farm in New Haven township, where he has since lived. Mr. Haber was married Nov. 30, 1872, to Miss Julia Friegel. To this union have been born six children, five of whom are now living. Mr. Haber assisted in clearing the farm which he now owns, and by years of hard work, has succeeded in making it one of the most attractive in the county.

Hamlin, L. W., the popular liveryman of Durand, is a native of this State. He was educated in the common schools, and has been engaged in his present line of business since 1890. Mr. Hamlin has one of the best equipped livery and sale stables in the county, and by energy and close attention to business has succeeded in building up a large trade.

Hamblin, Lawrence A., the junior member of the firm of Hamblin & Van Dusen, real estate and insurance agents of Owosso, Mich. Mr. Hamblin was born at Port Byron, N. Y., 1845. He received his education in a private school, and in 1865 came to Owosso where he has since resided. He first engaged in the foundry and machine business, and subsequently entered the employ of the government as railway postal clerk. In 1874 he was appointed postmaster at Owosso, and served as such for ten years. At the close of that period he engaged in the wholesale tobacco business, which he conducted three years. Mr. Hamblin then organized the present firm of Hamblin & Van Dusen, which is now doing an extensive business in insurance and real estate. Mr. Hamblin has always taken an active interest in politics, and is recognized as one of the leaders of the Republican party in this county. He has ever been ready to assist any enterprise that promised to be for the good of Owosso, and many of the homes and residences of the city have been erected by him.

Hartwell, Harmon, one of Durand's best-known citizens, was born at Geneva, N. Y., March 4, 1854. His father died when he was four years of age. Mr. Hartwell made his home with Mr. Solam Stone, and remained with him for twenty-five years. In company with that gentleman he came to Michigan. In 1853 he purchased a farm in Vernon township, which he operated for eleven years; since that time he has been a resident of Durand. He was married April 5, 1875, to Miss Jennie Wolf, who was also a native of New York. They are the parents of one child, a son. Mr. and Mrs. Hartwell are well known in Durand, and have many warm friends.

Hartwell, James H., the present postmaster of Hartwellville postoffice, and a well-known resident of Shiawassee township, was born at Sherburne, Chenango Co., New York, Dec. 22, 1824. He came with his parents to Michigan in the spring of 1836. They settled on a farm in Bennington township, a part of which he now owns and resides upon. He was one of the first school-teachers in Shiawassee county, and first began teaching in Antrim township. He was married in March, 1849, to Sarah S. Steuart. To this union has been born one daughter, now Mrs. F. C. Greenman. From 1850 to 1860 Mr. Hartwell conducted a general store, and later engaged in the sale of agricultural implements, which he followed successfully until 1878. Since that time he has given his whole attention to farming. He has filled the position of postmaster at Hartwellville since 1850 continuously, with the exception of one year; was elected supervisor of Bennington township, in 1865, and served as such for a number of years, he also filled the same office in Shiawassee township for two years. Mr. Hartwell is a member of the I. O. O. F. and of the Good Templars, and is one of the charter members of Crystal Fount lodge No. 11, which was established October 18, 1854, and is now the oldest lodge in the State. He has always taken an active interest in public affairs, and is well known throughout the country.

Hadsall, Henry S., attorney at law, at Owosso, Mich., and the junior member of the law firm of Lyon & Hadsall, is a native of New York State, having been born in Genesee country in 1858. When eight years of age his parents moved to Shiawassee county, Mich., and located at Byron, and it was in the schools of this county that he received his education. After completing his education, he moved to Tuscola county, Mich., and there followed school-teaching for some time. Mr. Hadsall began reading law at Vassar, Mich., and was admitted to practice in that county (Tuscola) in March, 1880. He practiced at Vassar until August, 1891, when he came to Owosso and formed a partnership with Mr. Gilbert R. Lyon, under the firm name of Lyon & Hadsall. During his residence in Tuscola county, Mr. Hadsall served as circuit court commissioner from 1885 to 1887; he has always taken an active interest in politics, and is an ardent Republican, and is now the nominee of that party for the office of mayor of Owosso. The firm of Lyon & Hadsall is one of the best known law firms in central Michigan, both gentlemen being recognized as able jurists.

Hall Brothers, wholesale and retail grocers of Owosso. The firm is composed of Mr. W. E. and Mr. L. C. Hall, and was organized in March, 1891. These gentlemen have both been life-long residents of Owosso, and received their education and business training in this city. They started business first as retailers, but in 1893 began wholesaling, purchasing their goods directly from the manufacturers, thus saving their customers the jobbers' profits. They carry a complete stock of groceries, and do an extensive business throughout this and adjoining counties. Mr. W. E. Hall, the senior member of the firm, is now serving as city treasurer of Owosso, and both of these gentlemen are well known and highly respected by the citizens of this city.

Hartshorn & Son, dealers in agricultural implements at Owosso, Mich. The senior member of the firm, Mr. A. E. Hartshorn, is a native of Vermont, having been born at Royalton in 1842. In 1855 he removed to Rochester, N. Y., where he remained until 1861. In that year he came to Shiawassee county, Mich., and purchased a farm in Bennington township, which he still owns. He followed farming as his occupation until 1882, when he came to Owosso and engaged in his present line of business. In 1890 he purchased the site of his present business, and erected the building he now occupies, and in that year formed a partnership with his son Fred E. He was married in 1863 to Miss Elvira Dolloff, a native of Ohio. They are the parents of three children, two daughters and one son, all of whom are now living. Mr. Hartshorn is a member of the I. O. O. F., and both he and wife are members of the Maple River Baptist church. This firm carries a general line of agricultural implements, seeds, etc., and does the most extensive business in the county.

Harris, J. B., farmer of Venice township, was born in Herkimer county, N. Y., in 1843. He came with his parents to Oakland county, Mich., when ten years of age, and resided in that county until 1882. In that year he purchased the farm in Venice township, where he now resides. He was married to Miss Eliza Ross, a resident of Oakland county, Mich. To this union have been born five children, four of whom are now living. Mr. Harris is one of the well-to do farmers of Venice township, and is the owner of one hundred and sixty acres of good land which is under a high state of cultivation.

Harrington, Fred M., a well-known insurance agent of Vernon, Mich., was born in Livingston county, this State, Sept. 1, 1871. He came with his parents to Bancroft when nine years of age, and was educated in the high school of Fenton. Mr. Harrington began the study of law in August, 1894, with Mr. A. J. Kellogg of Durand. He is now located at Vernon, where he is doing an extensive insurance business, and also pursuing the study of his chosen profession.

Huffman, J. J., was born in the township of Edenburgh, Portage county, O., May 4, 1841. He moved with his parents to Hancock county in 1845, where he received a common-school education, working in summer and attending school during winter. In August, 1861, he enlisted in the service of his country in the 49th Ohio Volunteer Infantry, serving four years and five months, during which time he was always with his command, never being off duty. His regiment belonged to the famous Army of the Cumberland, which was noted for its hard fighting, and never knew what it was to be whipped. In September, 1866, he was married to Sarah J. Frick. The fruits of this marriage were two daughters, Lilian G. and Ada M. He is a Republican politically, and was elected assessor in Washington township, Hancock county, O., in 1876. He moved to Michigan in 1878, and settled in the township of Rush, Shiawassee county, where he has held the office of treasurer for four years; and has been school director sixteen years, which office he still holds. April 6, 1889, he joined the Independent Order of Odd Fellows, and is a Past Grand. September, 1891, he joined the Knights of the Maccabees, holding a certificate of $2000.

Haughton, David, farmer of Woodhull township, was born in this State, in 1840. He came from Milford, Oakland county, where he was born, to Shiawassee, over twenty-five years ago, and has been a resident of this township since that time. Mr. Haughton was united in marriage in 1864 to Miss Amanda Smith. To this union have been born seven children, six sons and one daughter. Mr. Haughton is the owner of one hundred and eighty-five acres of good farming land, which is under a high state of cultivation. He was elected justice of the peace in Woodhull, in the spring of 1894. He has just been chosen by the people of this township to fill the office of supervisor, to which he was elected by a handsome majority. He is well known throughout the township and has many warm friends.

Haver, Eugene, farmer of Vernon township, was born Dec. 21, 1861, at Milford, Oakland county, Mich. He is a son of Jonathan Haver, who was born in New York State, in 1711, and who died in Shiawassee county, Mich., Jan. 8, 1889. Mr. Haver was united in marriage to Miss Libbie Reed, who was born in Vernon township, Feb. 8, 1861. She was the daughter of William J. Reed, who came to Michigan in 1836, and settled in this county. Mr. Haver is one of the well-known farmers of Shiawassee county, and has a wide circle of acquaintances and many warm friends.

High, Hiram R., attorney of Ovid, Mich., was born in 1860. Mr. High began the practice of law in 1886, and has followed that profession continuously at Ovid since that time. He was married April 11, 1886, to Miss Helena B. Everett, and to this union has been born one child. Mr. High is a member of the Masonic fraternity and a Knight Templar. He has always taken an active interest in judicial politics, but has never asked for himself a nomination to any office.

Hollister, Henry L., farmer of Venice township, was born in Wayne county, N. Y., in 1840. He continued to reside in his native State until he was fifteen years of age, when he came to Clinton county, Mich. At the breaking out of the war he enlisted in the 1st Michigan Cavalry in August, 1861, and served until 1865. He participated in many of the battles of the late war, and at the close of the same, was transferred to the western slope, where he remained one year. Mr. Hollister was married in October, 1866, to Miss Jennie Jagger. To this union were born seven children. His wife died in April, 1893. He was again married, March 21, 1895, to Mrs. J. L. Martin. Mr. Hollister has been a resident of this county since 1871. He now owns one hundred and twenty acres of good land, and is considered one of the well-to-do farmers of the county.

Horsman, Thomas J., attorney at law at Owosso, Mich., was born in Amherstburg, Ont., Feb. 10, 1848. He came to Michigan with his parents at the age of eight years, locating first at Adrian, and afterward moving to Detroit. In 1871 he came to Owosso, and followed the trade of a marble cutter for some years. In 1891 he began the study of law in the office of S. S. Smith of this city and was admitted to practice Sept. 1893. Mr. Horsman served as supervisor of the first district of Owosso for a number of years, and was nominated for prosecuting attorney on the Democratic ticket, for which he made a very creditable race. Although Mr. Horsman has followed the practice of law but a short time, he has already built up an extensive business, and is one of the rising attorneys of the bar.

Hutchings, Edward, proprietor of Hutchings' Sample Room at Bancroft, Mich., was born May 7, in this State, in 1858. He was educated in the common schools, and opened his present line of business when he was twenty-one years of age. Mr. Hutchings is also interested in the livery firm of Hutchings and Britten, who conduct a first-class livery and sale stable at Bancroft. Their rigs are first class throughout, and they enjoy a large trade.

Hutchings, Ruben, veterinary and farmer, of Shiawassee township, is a native of this county, having been born in Bennington township, Oct. 14, 1838. His early life was spent with his parents on a farm, and at the age of twenty-one he began learning the milling business. Mr. Hutchings first began business for himself by purchasing the grist-mill at Newburg, in company with George Cruthers. They operated this mill until 1879, when it was destroyed by fire. Since that time Mr. Hutchings has practiced as a veterinary surgeon, and followed farming in Shiawassee township. He was married Dec. 12, 1867, to Miss Nettie Diamond, who was born in the State of Wisconsin. To this union have been born three children, all of whom are now living. Mr. Hutchings and family are pleasantly situated on their farm in Shiawassee township, and their house is one of the most attractive in the county.

Hutchings, J. Harvey, the leading druggist of Bancroft, was born in Niagara county, N. Y., May 17, 1860. He was educated in the academy at Wilson and Columbia College of New York City. Mr. Hutchings was united in marriage to Sarah E. Abbott, a resident of this State, and to them have been born two children, Claud and Harvey. Mr. Hutchings is now serving the people of Bancroft as justice of the peace, and has also filled the office of village trustee. He is recognized as one of the best druggists in the county, and enjoys a large trade in Bancroft and throughout the surrounding country.

Jackson, Andrew, chief engineer of the city waterworks of Owosso. Our subject was born in Corunna, Mich., Nov. 18, 1852, and was educated in the schools of that city. At the age of thirteen he entered the employ of J. M. Thayer of that place, who was conducting a sash, door, and blind factory, and remained with him for some years. He later moved to Owosso and entered the employ of the Woodard Furniture Co., and for seventeen years had entire charge of steam plant and glazing department of that establishment. This position he resigned in order to accept the one he is now filling. Mr. Jackson was married Nov. 28, 1878 to Miss Jennie E. Camp of Byron. To this union have been born two daughters, both of whom are now living. He and wife are members of the M. E. Church; he is also a member of the A. O. U. W. and a charter member of the Owosso association of stationary engineers. Mr. Jackson is well known in Owosso and has many friends throughout the city.

Jacobs, William E., present sheriff of Shiawassee county, was born in Rutland county, Vt., in 1840. Came to Michigan in 1848 and to Shiawassee county in 1866. Mr. Jacobs has followed lumbering and farming as an occupation through life. At the breaking out of the late war he enlisted in Company K of the 16th Michigan Infantry and with that regiment participated in many of the hard fought battles of the war. He is a member of the H. F. Wallace Post G. A. R. and of the David West Commandery of the Union Veteran Union. Mr. Jacobs served the people of his township as supervisor for six years and in other minor offices. In 1892 he was nominated by the Republicans of his county for sheriff. He was elected by a large majority, and re-elected to the same office in 1894, the duties of which he is now discharging. As an officer, Mr. Jacobs has given entire satisfaction to the people, and his straightforward manner has won for him the respect and confidence of the entire county.

Johnson, Miss Edith M. The subject of this sketch is well known to the people of Venice township, having been born in this township in 1871, and is a daughter of Hiram and Frances Johnson of this county. Miss Johnson was educated in the district schools and finished her education by a course in the Vernon high school, graduating from the latter in 1890. She then found employment as a teacher, and has successfully taught for eight terms. She is at present employed by District No. 1 of Venice township, and has given complete satisfaction to the patrons of that district.

Johnson, A. V., farmer of Caledonia township, is a native of Lorain county, Ohio, having been born at Amherst that county, Sept. 18, 1837. In 1865, Mr. Johnson came to Michigan and purchased an eighty-acre farm between the cities of Owosso and Corunna, a part of which he has since platted and sold off in lots. These lots have found a ready sale, and occupy one of the most desirable locations along the line of the Owosso and Corunna street railway. Mr. Johnson was united in marriage, Aug. 30, 1862, to Miss Geneos Stewart. To this union has been born one child, a son. He has always taken an active interest in all public affairs, and is known as one of the public spirited and enterprising men of the county.

Jopling, William, V. S., the leading liveryman of Owosso, was born in Port Hope, Ont., in 1856. He came to Michigan in 1884 and located at Owosso where he began the practice of his profession, that of a veterinary surgeon. Mr. Jopling is a graduate of the agricultural college at Guelph, Ont., finishing there in 1879. He afterward attended the Ontario veterinary college, graduating from there in 1883. Mr. Jopling is a member of the Michigan State Veterinary Medical Association, which he has served as secretary for the past three years. He is also a member of the U. S. Veterinary Medical Association, and is now serving as State secretary for that organization. In August 1894, he purchased a livery stock at Owosso, where he is now doing a nice business, in connection with his veterinary practice. He was married in 1885 to Miss Jewel Pake, a resident of Bellville, Ont. To this union have been born two daughters.

Kellogg, A. J., attorney at law, Durand, Mich., was born at Milan, Cuyhoga Co., Ohio, July 1856. He came to Michigan in 1867, in company with his widowed mother, and located near Hastings, moving from there to Jackson in 1869, remaining in the latter place until 1870, when he moved to Corunna. He enlisted in the Regular Army, Company E, 1st U. S. Infantry, in 1879, serving two years with this company, when he was discharged for disabilities received on the Rio Grande River in Texas, being a non-commissioned officer at that time. He returned to Corunna and Dec. 28, 1882, was united in marriage to Ella G. Tears. He followed farming in New Haven township from 1886 to 1891; returning to Corunna he began the study of law with John T. McCurdy, and was admitted to the bar in 1893, when he immediately began practice at Durand, and was soon appointed village attorney. His business was good from the beginning and has been rapidly increasing.

Kendall, Simeon B., a well-known resident of Perry, Mich., was born in Stafford, Genesee Co., N. Y., Jan. 25, 1820. In Sept. 1882, he came to Genesee county, Michigan. At the breaking out of the war, Mr. Kendall enlisted, July 13, 1861, in Company A, 7th Wisconsin Infantry, which was a part of the 3rd division of the 4th army corps. He participated in the battles of Bull Run, South Mountain, Antietam, and Gainsville, Va., where he was severely wounded Aug. 28, 1862, in the left leg; this resulted in paralysis of the left leg and hip. He was taken to the Frederick City hospital, where he remained for two months; he was discharged Nov. 16, 1862. Mr. Kendall was married Jan. 1, 1860, to Elizabeth Osburn, a native of Poughkeepsie, N. Y. To this union have been born two children. Mr. Kendall is a member of Crawford Post, No. 310, and makes his home near the village of Perry.

Kerry, Samuel H., farmer and hay buyer of Caledonia township, was born in Oakland county this State. When two years of age, came with his parents to Shiawassee county, where he has since resided. Mr. Kerry has followed farming as an occupation through life, and for the past three years has bought and shipped large quantities of hay from this section of the country, shipping on an average of over three thousand tons per year. He has served the people as township clerk and two terms as school inspector. He is a member of the K. of M. and well known throughout the county.

Kilden, Bernard, one of the rising young law students of Corunna, was born in Venice township this county, March 1, 1867. Was educated in the Sandwich college; graduated from there in 1893. Began the study of law under the direction of John G. Knight Feb. 5, 1893, and with whom he is now studying. Mr. Kilden is a young man possessing more than ordinary ability, and we predict for him a bright future in the field of his chosen profession.

Kilburn, Newell, farmer of New Haven township, was born in Oswego county, N. Y., Jan. 2, 1821. He came to Michigan in 1865, and settled on a farm in New Haven township, where he remained through life. Mr. Albert Kilburn, the son of Newell Kilburn was also born in Oswego county N. Y., on Feb. 13, 1854. He was united in marriage Feb. 17, 1880, to Miss Louisa Bennett, and now resides on the old homestead in New Haven township. Mr. Kilburn is a thorough farmer and is well known and highly respected throughout the township.

Kilpatrick, Hon. William, attorney at law and the present State senator from Shiawassee county, is a native of Yates county, N. Y., having been born in the town of Middlesex, that county, Dec. 25, 1840. The early years of his life were spent on a farm and attending the common schools of that State. In 1860, he entered the Genesee Seminary, Lima, N. Y., and remained there until 1865. In that year he removed to Illinois, and taught school for one year in that State. In 1864 he entered the law department of the Michigan University at Ann Arbor, graduating from there in 1866. He at once began to practice at Owosso, and has followed his business here continuously since that time. He served the people as city attorney from 1869 to 1873, and as supervisor at large, from 1873 to 1875; was elected mayor of Owosso in 1875, declining a renomination in 1876. This same year Mr. Kilpatrick was elected prosecuting attorney for the county, and re-elected in 1878. He resigned this office in 1880, in order that he might make the race for State senator, from the old 17th district, which then comprised the counties of Livingston and Shiawassee, to which office he was elected. In 1881, in company with Mr. M. L. Stewart, he engaged in the general banking business at Owosso, and erected the present bank block on the corner of Washington and Exchange streets. In 1883, he disposed of his interest in the banking business, and

COUNTY BUILDINGS.

OWOSSO CHURCHES.

MAPLE RIDGE PARK.

OWOSSO has many things in which she takes a just amount of pride, yet we doubt if there is any one thing that is so often pointed out to strangers and remarked upon for its rapid growth, central location, well-graded streets, and number of comfortable and modern homes as "the MAPLE RIDGE PARK" addition to the city. This tract of land was known for years as the Keyte farm, and contains eighty acres of land. It was owned for many years by Moses Keyte, an old resident of Owosso, and the pioneer harness-maker of the place. Nov. 1, 1893, its improvements consisted of a barn and a board fence. At this time it was purchased by its present owners, Messrs. Lingle & McDannel, who at once began platting the land and clearing away the underbrush. As soon as they had completed this work, they set out over a thousand hard-maple shade trees, and the following spring began the grading of streets, and that summer completed over a thousand rods of well-graded streets. The sale of lots, however, had commenced the previous January, William Eggleston being the first purchaser, buying lots thirty-two and thirty-three in block two, where he at once began the erection of a house, which was the first one built on this addition. The sale of lots was rapid from this time on, and in the first year over three hundred and twenty-five lots were sold and thirty-five houses erected.

The development of this part of the city is due largely to the energy and push of these two young men, Messrs. Lingle & McDannel. The senior member of the firm, Mr. William H. Lingle, is a native of Ohio, having been born in Henry county, near the village of Wauseon, July 28, 1867. Here his early life was passed. He received a common school education in the schools of Delta and Wauseon. In 1885 his parents came to Michigan and purchased a farm near Owosso. Mr. Lingle began life as a school teacher, and followed this occupation for two years; he then entered a Detroit business college, and from there entered the employ of the Estey Manufacturing Company of this city as stenographer. He continued in the employ of this company for over two years, resigning this position to accept that of chief clerk to the superintendent of the Toledo & Ann Arbor R. R., and remained in the employ of this company until Dec. 1, 1893, when he resigned his position, so that he might give his whole time and attention to the development of MAPLE RIDGE PARK Jan. 1, 1890. Mr. Lingle was married to Miss Mabel A. Cooper, who was born and raised in Shiawassee county, and comes from one of the oldest families of the county; is eldest daughter of D. C. Cooper, the present clerk of this county.

Mr. Frank J. McDannel, the junior member of this firm, is a native of Indiana, being born in De Kalb county, that State, near the village of Butler, Feb. 18, 1864. While he was quite young, his parents moved to Ohio and settled near Bryan. Mr. McDannel was educated in the schools of that place, and at an early age learned telegraphy, entering the employ of the Lake Shore & Michigan Southern R. R., first as messenger boy, and from that position worked his way step by step to that of train despatcher, which he held for five years, at Toledo, Ohio, resigning to accept position as chief train despatcher with the Toledo & Ann Arbor R. R., which he resigned that he might give his whole time and attention to the new enterprise, the business having assumed such proportions by this time that one man was unable to attend to it. Feb. 17, 1892, Mr. McDannel married Miss Hattie May Cooney, of Bryan, Ohio, the daughter of Dr. H. Cooney, a prominent physician and druggist of that place.

Both of these gentlemen have been untiring in their efforts to make MAPLE RIDGE PARK the most attractive part of Owosso. The land has a number of natural advantages which are not found in any other part of the city: over twenty flowing wells have already been found, the water is clear as crystal and as cold as ice, and rises in a number of places over two feet above the level of the ground. Their land is crossed by both the T. & A. A. R. R. and the D. G. H. & M. R. R., while running directly in front of it is the Owosso & Corunna street railway, which give the residents of this addition every advantage. MAPLE RIDGE PARK we firmly believe is destined to become the most attractive resident portion of Owosso; the company intend to soon platt and open for sale "MAPLE RIDGE HEIGHTS," which is a beautiful piece of land lying just back of the Park. To the prospective purchaser of a home in Owosso, we have this advice to offer: Before buying land elsewhere, go to MAPLE RIDGE PARK, see, and become convinced that this is now, and will certainly continue to be, the most beautiful residence part of Owosso.

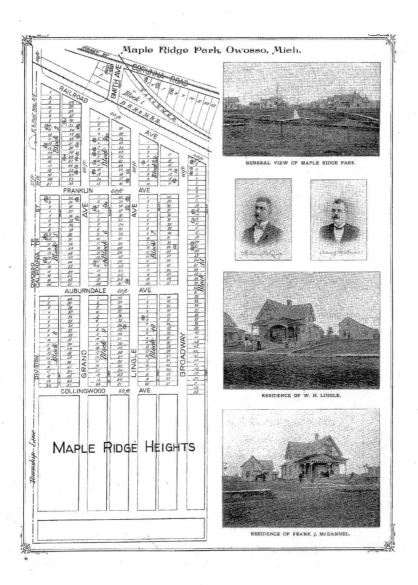

Maple Ridge Park, Owosso, Mich.

GENERAL VIEW OF MAPLE RIDGE PARK.

RESIDENCE OF W. H. LINGLE.

RESIDENCE OF FRANK J. McDANNEL.

MAPLE RIDGE HEIGHTS

McLain, George W. This gentleman is the well-known furniture dealer and funeral director of Durand. He was born in Cayuga county, N. Y., in the town of Sterling, Oct. 25, 1839, and at the age of seven years, he moved with his parents to Michigan, and settled on

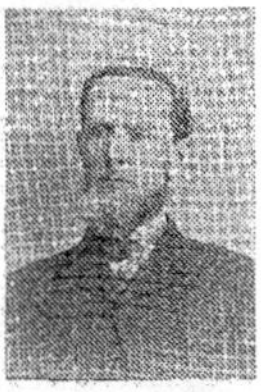

what is now known as the Crapo farm, in Genesee county, Mich. Jan. 1, 1857, he was united in marriage to Miss Catherine Angus, eldest daughter of Bradley and Mary Angus, a resident of Tyrone, Livingston county, this State, March 1, 1887. Mr. McLain engaged in his present line of business at Chesaning, Saginaw Co., this State, and followed it there until Aug. 14, 1889; in that year he came to Durand and founded his present business. Mr. McLain has made a careful study of his line and by so doing has succeeded in building up a large and profitable business. As a funeral director and embalmer he is excelled by none.

Mc Laughlin, H. B., a well-known merchant of Vernon, was born in the State of New York, June 23, 1851. He came to Michigan with his parents when yet a child, and first located at Corunna, where the early years of his life were spent. He first began business as a clerk and was employed both at Corunna and at this place for a period of four years. At the end of that time he organized the firm of Holmes & Mc Laughlin, and engaged in the sale of dry goods and groceries. This firm did business for over ten years, when Mr. Mc Laughlin disposed of his interest therein, and opened a stock of dry goods, boots and shoes, etc., which business he is now operating. He carries a complete line in all departments, and has by close attention to business and fair dealing built up a trade of which he is justly proud.

Mc Bride, Walter, attorney at law at Corunna, was born in Caledonia township, this county, Jan. 13, 1869. He is a son of Albert R. Mc Bride, now deceased, who was a prominent attorney at Corunna from 1875 until the time of his death in January 1894. He served as prosecuting attorney for three terms and as supervisor for nine years. At the breaking out of the war, Albert Mc Bride enlisted in the 10th Michigan Cavalry as a member of Company F, and served two years with that organization. Our subject was educated in the schools of Corunna and began the study of law in 1889 in his father's office, being admitted to practice before the supreme court, Jan. 17, 1890; he has followed his profession since that time at Corunna. Mr. Mc Bride has been successful in the practice of law, and is one of the rising young attorneys of Shiawassee county.

Mc Clintock, Gilman J., present postmaster of Laingsburg, Mich., was born in Wayne county, N. Y., Sept. 17, 1832. He moved from there to the State of Ohio in 1836, and resided there until 1851. In that year he came to Michigan, and has been a resident of this State since that time. During the late war Mr. Mc Clintock served from 1861 to July 1862 as 1st. Lieut. in Company D, of the 14th Michigan Infantry. He was united in marriage in 1851 to Miss Wealthy Ann Marshall. To this union have been born seven children, one son and six daughters. Mr. Mc Clintock has served the people of Laingsburg four terms as supervisor, four years as town clerk, and has held four commissions as postmaster. He has been before the people as a candidate for representative, county clerk, and registrar of deeds. He is well known to the people of Laingsburgh and surrounding country, and enjoys the respect and confidence of all.

Mc Curdy, John T., attorney at law of Corunna, Mich., was born in that city in 1860. He is the son of the Hon. Hugh M. Mc Curdy, a sketch of whom appears elsewhere in this work. Our subject was educated in the schools of Corunna, and completed his education by a course at the military academy at Suspension Bridge, N. Y. He began the study of law in Corunna in 1878, and was admitted to the bar in Dec., 1881. He began to practice at Corunna in 1883 and has followed it here continuously since that time. Mr. Mc Curdy has by industry and close attention to business built up a large practice and is recognized as one of the leaders in his profession. He holds the position of local attorney for the C. & G. T. system of railway in this county, and also attorney for the First National Bank of Corunna.

Mc Kay, Arthur, a well-known merchant at New Lothrop, was born at Vittoria, Norfolk Co., Ontario, Jan. 25, 1852. Came to Michigan in 1877 and located at New Lothrop, where he engaged in business with Mr. C. K. Runnells. He afterward purchased the business and then organized the firm of Viets & Mc-Kay. To this business he succeeded and is now doing an extensive trade. He later disposed of an interest in the business to Mr. Mott, and the firm is now known as Mc Kay and Mott. They carry a general line of groceries, dry goods, boots and shoes, hardware, gent's furnishing goods, and all goods kept in a first-class general store. They have by courteous treatment and fair dealing built up a large trade, and the firm is well known throughout this and adjoining towns.

Marsh, H & R., farmers of Bennington township. They located on this farm in 1846, and since that time have been engaged in farming and general stock raising. In 1890, they became more extensively interested in the breeding of fine Rambouillet sheep. They have followed farming as an occupation through life and have been unusually successful.

Michigan Sewing Machine & Organ Co., one of Owosso's leading business enterprises, was established over twenty-five years ago, and since that time has been doing an extensive business through the central part of the State. It is divided into four departments; viz., pianos, organs, sewing machines, and bicycles. This

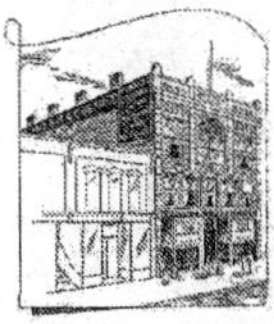

house handles a large variety of high and medium grade goods, and a large quantity disposed of each year gives them a decided advantage over their competitors. Messrs. Shattuck are well known in Owosso, and have filled several responsible official positions. They have enlarged their business from year to year until now it is one of the largest of its kind in the State.

Miner, Selden S., one of the best-known attorneys of Owosso, Mich., was born in Livingston county, June 5, 1854. He was educated first in the schools of Corunna and completed his education by a course in the law department at the university at Ann Arbor. He was admitted to practice in the supreme court in 1878. The following May he began the practice of his profession, which he followed for a year at Corunna, when he moved to Flushing, remaining at the later place but a few months, when he returned to Corunna and continued to reside there until 1892. In that year he came to Owosso, and has practiced here since that time. Mr. Miner has served the people in various official capacities, first as circuit court commissioner in 1878, and again in 1880. In the spring of 1884 he was elected to that office at the end of three years. In 1888 he was supervisor of the second ward of Corunna; resigning, elected mayor of Corunna and served in that capacity for one year. He also served as a member of the school board for five years. Mr. Miner was elected prosecuting attorney for this county in 1888, and ably discharged the duties of this office for four years. He is a member of the Masonic fraternity and also of the K. of P's. He is well known throughout this and adjoining counties and enjoys a large practice.

Miller, Fredrick, farmer of Bennington township, was born in Germany, June 21, 1835. The early years of his life were spent in the baking business with his father, which profession he followed in his native land until 1856, when he came to the United States and first settled in Waterloo, Ontario, where he found employment as a farm laborer, and which he followed until May 20, 1859. In that year he came to Washtenaw county, Mich., where he resided until May, 1864. At that time he came to Bennington, Shiawassee county, and purchased a part of the farm which he now owns, and to which he has added from time to time until he is now the possessor of one of the best farms in Shiawassee county.

Martin, John Y., of Caledonia township, was born in this township, June 8, 1863, on the farm that he now owns. He is a son of Eli Martin and the grandson of Samuel S. Martin who was one of the pioneers of this county. Our subject received his education in the common schools of the county and in the Corunna high school. Followed teaching for some time, but has followed farming as an occupation the greater part of his life. He was married April 24, 1890, to Miss Lillian M. Holley, daughter of Dr. D. C. Holley at Vernon. To this union have been born two sons, one of whom is now living. Mr. Martin has served the people as township treasurer for four years, and has also filled the office of justice of the peace, and is now serving his third time as supervisor. In all offices he has filled, he has given entire satisfaction to the people.

Moore, Nathan, farmer of Hazelton township, was born near Auburn, Cayuga Co., N. Y., July 11, 1846. He came with his parents to Michigan when six years of age, and first located in Genesee county, where they resided for ten years. From there he came to Hazelton township and settled on section 31. He was united in marriage Dec. 24, 1875, to Miss Ellen Sherman, who was born in Franklin county, N. Y., Oct. 5, 1855. To this union have been born two children, William H., March 12, 1878, and Frank L., Aug. 9, 1881. Mr. Moore is engaged in farming and also in the sale of the Butler windmill of which he has sold a large number throughout the county. He also handles the Empire binders and mowers. He has a large acquaintance throughout the county and many warm personal friends.

Moyses, J. H., farmer of Venice township, was born in Cambridgeshire, England, March 18, 1832, and has been a resident of Shiawassee county, since March, 1866. He served in the British Army from 1850 to 1860 and was awarded the silver medal by the queen of England for bravery and meritorious conduct during the Sepoy war of 1857 to 1858. He came to the United States in 1860 and in 1861 enlisted in the 28th New York Infantry and served as a member of that regiment through the War of the Rebellion. He received three gun-shot wounds at Slaughter, Nelson Co., Va., Aug. 9, 1862, and was held as prisoner of war both in Libby prison and at Belle Isle.

A detailed account of Mr. Moyses's service as a soldier both in this and his native land would no doubt prove intensely interesting to the people of this county, and we regret that limited space will not permit. Suffice it to say that both as a soldier and citizen he stands in the front ranks to-day.

Mumby, Walter H., cigar manufacturer of Corunna, was born in Pontiac, Oakland Co., Mich., July 14, 1862. He came to Owosso when ten years of age. After acquiring his education and trade of cigar making, he located in Corunna in 1884 as a manufacturer of cigars, with but small capital; by careful and faithful attention to his business, he soon enjoyed a paying and extensive trade, and established a reliable reputation and demand for his cigars. Mr. Mumby purchased his present location in 1888, and now has a large trade throughout the State, making some of the best known

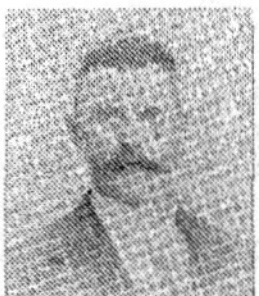

brands on the market, among which can be mentioned the "Mumby" and the "Martino," both recognized as standard cigars in their respective fields. Mr. Mumby has served his city as city recorder, city treasurer, and is now on his fifth year as alderman — being a careful and painstaking official, always alert to the interests of his city.

Morris, Francis H., the present supervisor of New Haven township, was born in Wayne county, Michigan, Aug. 11, 1850, where he resided until 1880. In that year he came to Shiawassee county and purchased a farm in New Haven township, where he now resides. He was married March 9, 1872, to Miss Melvine Postiff, who was born in France, Oct. 18, 1851, and came with her parents to America when two years of age. To this union were born six children, three sons and three daughters, all of whom are now living. Mr. Morris has served the people of his township as township treasurer for two years, as supervisor for four years, and as a member of the school Board for six years. He is an ardent prohibitionist and is recognized as one of the leaders of that party in this county.

Murlin, Desmond, farmer of Vernon township, was born in Oakland county, Mich., March 19, 1832. He resided with his parents until twenty-two years of age, when he came to Vernon, Shiawassee county, and purchased a farm, at that time an untrodden wilderness. Through his industry it is now one of the best improved farms in the county. He was married Jan. 6, 1864, to Mary C. Barton, who was born in Monroe county, N. Y., Oct. 18, 1829. Mr. and Mrs. Murlin are members of the Congregational Church, and are highly respected throughout the township.

National Tag Company, The. Mr. C. R. Crane, inventor of this tag, and manager of the above-named company located at Durand, Mich., has, by patient industry and push in the face of obstacles and discouragements that would have driven to the wall a man of

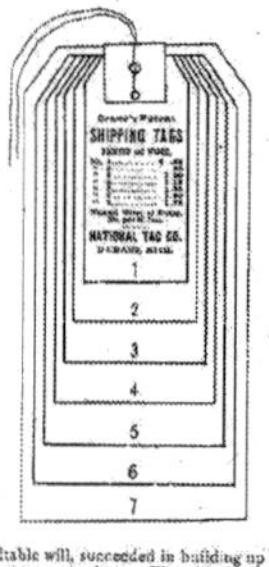

less indomitable will, succeeded in building up his present and prosperous business. The vicissitudes through which Mr. Crane has passed in his struggles against time and tide remind one who has read the lives of Elias Howe, Goodyear, Morse, etc., of the trials and difficulties which they so successfully overcame in placing before the world the products of their genius.

Olney, J. C., farmer of Venice township, was born in the State of New York, Nov. 23, 1863, and came to Michigan in 1885. In 1887 he was united in marriage to Miss Marie Martin, the daughter of James Martin, a well-known resident of Laingsburg. Mr. Olney is the owner of one hundred and twenty acres of land, which is under a high state of cultivation, and he is considered one of the progressive farmers of the township.

Osburn & Sons. This firm is probably the oldest business house in the city of Owosso, having been established in 1857 by Mr. John M. Osburn. They carry a complete line of dry goods, carpets, etc., and also a general line of clothing and gent's furnishing goods. They occupy both floors and basement of a large double store, and employ over twenty people. This firm buys all of their goods for spot cash, and are thus enabled to give their customers the benefit of a cash purchase. Their stock is complete in every department, and they are perhaps to-day the best known firm in Shiawassee county. They have a large business which they conduct on the one-price system in this and adjoining counties.

Owen, George W., editor of the *Shiawassee American,* was born in Monroe county, Michigan, Feb. 15, 1840. At the the age of fifteen he entered the office of the *Monroe Commercial,* where he remained until the breaking out of the war, when he enlisted in Company A, Fourth Michigan Infantry, and served with that organization until Feb. 26, 1866, when he was mustered out at San Antonia, Texas. He participated in all battles in which his regiment engaged, to the number of about one hundred, and was wounded several times, but not seriously. He was present at the famous surrender of Lee, and belonged to the brigade that received the arms and colors of Lee's army. At the close of the war, he returned to Detroit, Mich., and worked as compositor on the *Detroit Post* for seven years. He then entered the employ of the *Tribune* and remained with them until 1870. In that year he moved to Owosso and began the publication of the *Shiawassee Republican,* which was consolidated with the *Shiawassee American,* in June 1886. Mr. Owen has been twice married, and is the father of five children, three of whom are now living. He is a member of the G. A. R., the I. O. O. F., and a number of other secret organizations. As an editor he is possessed of rare ability, and the *Shiawassee American* is a bright and newsy sheet.

Owosso Land, Lumber, and Fuel Co. (Limited). This company was organized Jan. 1, 1894, and is composed of the following well-known gentlemen: Mr. D. M. Estey, George B. Symes, and F. T. Harris. This company does an extensive business, and each year purchases and clears large tracts of timber land in this State. All of these gentlemen have for a number of years been residents of Owosso, and their genial manner and winning ways have won for them a host of friends throughout the State.

Owosso Savings Bank, The. This well-known banking house was organized in January, 1891, and succeeded the old Second National Bank, which was established in 1886. It has a capital stock of $100,000 and a surplus of $17,000, pays four per cent interest on saving deposits, and has declared four per cent semi-annual dividends since its organization. The original banking house was on the corner of Washington and Mason streets, but they were compelled to remove to new quarters on account of increasing business, and consequently purchased the Sharpstene block which they now own and occupy. It is well equipped with a steel vault, nine by sixteen feet, and seven feet high. The doors and vestibules weigh five tons each. The safety deposit section of the vault has a capacity of one thousand boxes. Its officers and directors are among Owosso's best known people: President, C. S. Williams; Vice President, Chas. E. Rigley; Cashier, A. D. Whipple; Asst. Cashier, John C. VanCamp. They do a general banking business and issue drafts on all parts of the world.

Owosso Times, The. This paper was established in 1889, by Mr. E. O. Dewey, the present editor and proprietor. The *Times* enjoys a circulation of over twenty-five hundred, and is a leading Republican paper of the county. Its editor, Mr. Dewey, is well known in Owosso and throughout the county, having served as secretary of the County Fair Association for the past ten years. It is well equipped with the most modern presses, and the paper presents a neat appearance and is bright and newsy throughout.

Park, H. N., & Son, the leading hardware firm of New Lothrop, was organized August 1894. The business, however, had been conducted at Flushing some twenty-five years by Mr. M. N. Park. They carry a complete stock of hardware in all branches and make a specialty of roofing and cavestroughing. Both of these gentlemen are expert tinners and thorough workmen in their line. They have by honesty and fair dealing succeeded in building up a large trade, and their business is excelled by few if any in the county.

Parsons, John, a farmer of Caledonia township, is a native of this State, having been born in Ionia county, Oct. 16, 1843. When five years of age, he removed with his father to Shiawassee county, remained here until eighteen years of age, when he returned to Ionia county, where he lived three years, when he returned to Shiawassee county and bought the farm in Caledonia township on which he now resides. He was married March 21, 1868, to Miss Katie R. Ormsby, who came from Jefferson county, New York in 1861. To this union have been born eight children, all of whom are now living. Besides conducting his farm, Mr. Parsons is largely interested in the manufacture of cider, vinegar and jelly. He has a well-arranged plant on his farm with the capacity of seventy-five barrels per day, and a cellar with a storage capacity of five hundred barrels. The products of this mill are of a superior grade and find a market throughout this and adjoining States.

Patterson, A. B., present proprietor of the National Hotel at Owosso, is a native of this city, having been born here in 1860. In 1870 his father purchased the National Hotel property which they have operated since that time. It is centrally located, has fifty sleeping rooms and also a good livery in connection with the house. The house is now doing a thriving business under the present management and is one of the leading hotels in the city.

Patchel, Peter, farmer of Vernon township, was born in the State of New Jersey, Aug. 22, 1844. When four years old, he came with his parents to Michigan and settled on a farm in Vernon township. Here he received his early education and assisted his father in clearing the old homestead. On reaching his majority, he assumed the management of the farm until the death of his father, March 18, 1891. He was married Feb. 19, 1868, to Miss Ann E. Jones. To this union have been born three children, a son and two daughters. He and wife are members of the church and are highly respected throughout the township.

Peacock, Ebenezer, farmer and stock raiser of Woodhull township, is a native of this State, having been born in Washtenaw county, in 1846. When he was a year and a half old his parents moved to Clinton county where our subject remained until 1891. In that year he came to Shiawassee county and located in Woodhull township, where he has followed farming and stock-buying successfully since that time. He was married twice having three children by his first wife. His present wife to whom he was married in 1888 was Miss Ina Bates, a native of Bedford, Monroe county. To this union have been born five children, four sons and a daughter, all of whom are now living. Mr. Peacock is well known in Woodhull township and throughout the county; he has been successful as a farmer and owns one of the best improved farms of the county.

Peck, Andrew, farmer of Hazelton township. Was born at Nelson, Matteson Co., N. Y., May 16, 1819. He continued to reside there until twenty-one years of age, and in 1852 came to Michigan and first located in Oakland county. From there he moved to Genesee county in 1853, where he remained for twenty-two years. After that, Mr. Peck resided at Flushing and from there came to Shiawassee county and settled in Hazelton township where he now resides. He was united in marriage to Miss Eunice M. Terry who was born in Wayne county, N. Y., Aug. 7, 1827. To this union have been born seven children, five of whom are now living. Besides carrying on general farming, Mr. Peck is interested with his son, Ira T., in the threshing business and does a good business in that line. His son, Ira T., was born in Genesee county, Oct. 6, 1855, and was married to Miss Nellie Michel, Jan. 2, 1881. His wife died March 14, 1882. Both he and his father are well known to the people of Hazelton township and enjoy the respect and confidence of all.

Perry, Forrest B., farmer of Hazelton township, was born in the town of Hadley, Lapeer Co., Mich., Nov. 5, 1856. Was educated in the common schools of his native county and continued to reside there until 1884, when he came to Hazelton township and purchased sixty acres of land on section 19 where he now resides. Was united in marriage Oct. 1, 1879, to Miss Elnora B. Addes, a native of Oakland county. To this union have been born two children, Floyd W., born December 4, 1884, and Roy, born Dec. 3, 1889. Mr. Perry has one of the finest homes in the township and enjoys a large acquaintance in the county.

Pearson, William, farmer of Venice township, was born in Northampton county, Pennsylvania, in 1843. Resided there until 1862 when he came to Oakland county, Michigan, where he remained until 1871. In that year he came to Venice township, this county. Mr. Pearson was married in 1873, to Miss Harriet M. Irwin. To this union have been born two children, both of whom are now living. Mr. Pearson has a comfortable home and his farm is under a high state of cultivation. He carries on general farming and gives special attention to the breeding of a high grade of stock.

Perry Village, situated on the C. & G. T. R. R., eighteen miles from Lansing, is one of the most thriving villages in central Michigan. It is located in a fine portion of the county for agricultural pursuits, has a population of about five hundred and fifty, and is a desirable town for a residence, having three flourishing churches, a good school, grist mill, saw mill, and a factory which promises to be one of the best of which Michigan can boast; viz., The Lamb Glove and Mitten Manufacturing Co.

The present village officers are: President, E. L. Watkins; trustees, Messrs. E. B. Davis, Cyrus Moore, L. C. Watkins, C. H. Stevens, E. A. Runyan, and E. A. Burke; clerk, H. H. Hawley; assessor, H. A. Spalding; street commissioner, G. W. Rolfe; marshall, Geo. Haskins; fire warden and engineer of fire department, J. M. Summers.

Peters, H. B., farmer of Fairfield township, was born in London, Eng., June 22, 1837. He came with his parents to Canada when two years of age, and removed from there to the United States, Oct. 28, 1879. They first settled in Lorain county, Ohio, and remained there for five years, coming to Michigan, in March, 1884, and settled in Saginaw county. In 1890, Mr. Peters came to Shiawassee county and purchased the farm which he now occupies. He was married in May,

1879, to Miss Elizabeth Curtiss. To this union have been born eight children, four sons and four daughters all of whom are living. Mr. Peters has by industry and economy succeeded in making for himself one of the most pleasant homes in Shiawassee county. He is a member of the K. O. T. M., Chapin Lodge 407, and is well known throughout the township.

Parker, Miles L., manufacturer of pressed and common brick, also well and drain tile, of Owosso, is a native of this State, having been born at Marion, Livingston county, June 1, 1848. Mr. Parker came to Shiawassee county with his parents,

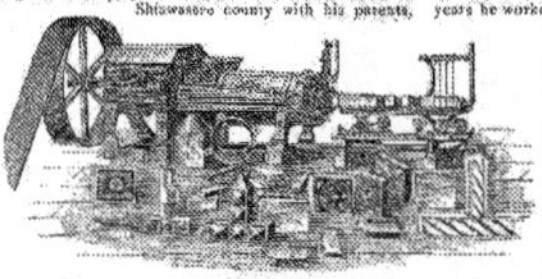

when nine years of age, and the early part of his life was spent on R. H. Hall's Brick yard in Spring Wells, Wayne county. At the age of sixteen he began work on a brick yard at Saginaw and followed that business in different parts of the country until 1874. In that year he came to Owosso and engaged as foreman on the Parker and Belford brick yard, which position he held for thirteen years. At that time Mr. Parker became proprietor of the plant he is now operating with improved machinery. He has always taken an active interest in public affairs and is now serving his third term as alderman for the fourth ward. He also served as turnkey under his father, who was sheriff of the county from 1864 to 1868. Mr. Parker was married in 1875 to Miss Naomi J. Warren, a native of this county. He is now doing an extensive business, and his products find a market in different parts of the State. He is well known to the people of Owosso, and is recognized as one of her most energetic and substantial business men. He is located at 822 S. Ceder street.

Parker, Charles W., the present supervisor of the first district of Owosso, and one of her best-known business men, is a native of this State, having been born in Livingston county, Feb. 27, 1851. In 1852 his parents removed to the city of Detroit and remained there until 1859, when his father came to Shiawassee county and purchased a farm in Antrim township, where he resided until his election as sheriff of the county in 1866, and to which he returned after the expiration of the term of his office. Our subject on reaching his majority, entered the employ of the M. C. R. R. at Detroit, and remained with that company for some time. Later he returned to Shiawassee county and engaged in the general mercantile business, which he has followed almost continuously in this county since that time, being now located in the Mason Block in West Owosso. Mr. Parker was married June 17, 1876, to Miss Ida Andrews, who died at Rome, Georgia, in 1883, Mr. Parker having been in the employ of the Ridge Valley Iron company at the time of her death. He immediately returned to Owosso and has been a resident of this city since that time. In politics, Mr. Parker is an ardent Republican, and during his services as supervisor, he has so discharged the duties of that office as to give complete satisfaction to all classes.

Pencock, James J., attorney at law and justice of the peace at the city of Corunna, was born in the township of Walworth, Wayne county, New York, Feb. 26, 1844. He continued to reside in his native State until the year 1855; when he came with his parents to Michigan, and located at Corunna, Shiawassee county. He received his education in the schools of that city. In August, 1862, he enlisted in Company H, 23rd Michigan Infantry, and served two years and four months. He was discharged from the service with the rank of corporal, on account of gun-shot wounds. He was twice wounded at the battle of Resaca, Georgia, in May, 1864. After his discharge from the service, he followed contracting and building. In 1888 he was admitted to practice in the department of the interior as a pension attorney, which he still follows. In 1893 he was elected justice of the peace, which he still holds. He is also supervisor of the third ward, city of Corunna, this being his fifth year in that capacity. Mr. Pencock is a member of the Union Veteran's Union; was elected first colonel of command No. 5, department of Michigan. He is also a member of the G. A. R.; and was three times elected commander of H. F. Wallace Post No. 160 Department of Michigan. He was admitted to the bar of Shiawassee county, Sept. 16, 1893; and although he has not practiced to any extent up to the present time, yet his advice is often sought in legal questions.

Phelps, H. H., son of Dyer and Almyra (Soddy) Phelps was born May 6, 1844, at the old homestead; his sister Eliza Jane, is the wife of Nucomb Mitchell, was born in Springfield, Pa., Dec. 25, 1835. His parents were among the first settlers purchasing land on section 20, Shiawassee county, where by persevering effort, the forest was transformed into a home of cheerful hospitality and comfort. The mother departed this life October, 1854. The father, January, 1875. Our subject remained at home with his parents until twenty-one years of age. July 2, 1865, he was married to Miss Edna Z. Hendee of Venice, Shiawassee Co. For three years he worked his father's farm on shares. In September, 1868, he purchased forty acres on section 30. He has subsequently added to this until now his farm comprises one hundred and thirty-eight acres. He spares no pains to improve and beautify his home. He and wife are members of the Maple River Baptist church and are highly respected throughout their township. The parents of Mrs. Phelps are also among the pioneers of the county, coming here in an early day and have resided here through life. Her father, W. B. Hendee, was born in Rutland county, Vt., Dec. 7, 1813, and her mother, Miss R. S. (Potter) Hendee was born in Niagara county, N. Y., March 6, 1818, and died in this State, Oct. 3, 1875. They were married October 9, 1836, and came to this State in 1839, locating in Venice township in 1850. To this union were born the following children: Elisabeth J., born June 3, 1838, died in September, 1838; Oscar F., born Aug. 21, 1839; Royal D., born Oct. 30, 1841 (killed at James Island, S. C., June 16, 1862); Edna Z., born April 8, 1844; Orlando J., born Jan. 25, 1847; Warren C., born Oct. 27, 1849, died Feb. 23, 1876; Ira B., born Oct. 5, 1852; Ida C., born Oct. 27, 1855, and Lena D., born Feb. 22, 1862.

Phippen, Samuel S. C., M. D., physician and surgeon of Owosso, Mich., was born in Brooklin, Ontario, March 26, 1862. He is the son of Nicholas Phippen, who did an extensive business in lumbering and the manufacture of furniture, in Ontario. Dr. Phippen received his education in the schools of his native county and at the Park Hill high school of Middlesex county, from which he graduated in 1876, receiving a first class teacher's certificate. He next matriculated before the college of physicians and surgeons of Ontario in August 1878, and became registered as an undergraduate in medicine in the university of Toronto, and later attended lectures at the Toronto school of medicine for one year. In order to complete his medical education, Dr. Phippen then studied one year with Dr. Walter Moorehouse, a celebrated physician of London, Canada; he then entered the medical department of Mc Gill University, from which he graduated in March 1883. He first began the practice of his profession at Owosso, Mich., in June, 1883, where he now resides. He was united in marriage September, 1886, to Miss Anna Kohler, a resident of Owosso, Mich. The doctor is a member of the Owosso academy of medicine, the Michigan State Medical Society, the American Medical Association, and the National Association of Railroad Surgeons. He holds the position of local surgeon for the M. C. R. R., and assistant surgeon of the 2nd regiment of the Michigan Brigade, of the uniform rank of the Knights of Pythias, which gives him the rank of captain on the colonel's staff. He is also a member of the Knights of the Maccabees and of Lansing Lodge Order of Elks. In 1893 Dr. Phippen was appointed a member of the Board of Pension Examiners and is now acting in that capacity. As a physician and surgeon, Dr. Phippen is held in high esteem by his brother practitioners, and enjoys a large and growing practice.

Phillips, Samuel, the leading groceryman of Lennon, was born in the State of Iowa in the year 1862, and resided here till eight years of age. He then came to Eaton county, Michigan, and from there to Lennon, where he is now engaged in the grocery business. Mr. Phillips was married in 1886 to Miss Margaret Shooks. To this union have been born four children, all of whom are now living. He is what can be called a self-made man, his father having died in 1864. He has been engaged in the grocery business since 1893 and has succeeded in building up a large trade.

Philips & Henry, the popular grocerymen of Bancroft. Mr. N. G. Philips, the senior member of this firm, was born at Bancroft, July 5, 1871, and has resided here during his entire life. Elbert Henry, the junior member of the firm, is a native of Livingston county, having been born in the town of Green Oak, Oct. 11, 1863. This firm succeeds F. L. Convis, and since purchasing the business, they have enlarged it in all departments and now carry the most complete line of grocery and bazaar goods in the county. Their trade is steadily increasing and they are now doing a large and profitable business.

Preece, Charles H., owner and proprietor of the Miller House of Owosso, was born in Alexander Bay, N. Y., in 1857. He resided in his native State until 1881, when he came to Owosso and purchased this hotel which he is now operating. He was married in 1885 to Miss Libbie Mansbart, a resident of this city. To this union have been born four children, all of whom are living. He is a member of the Masonic Fraternity and the K. of P's, and is well known in Owosso.

Purvas, Alex., farmer of Owosso township, was born near Toronto, Canada, Jan. 17, 1841. He was educated in the schools of his native land, remaining there until twenty-four years of age, when he came to Michigan in 1865 and purchased one hundred acres of land in this township which he cleared and improved. He was united in marriage to Miss Mary A. Ockerman, also a native of Canada, born near the town of Percy, March 6, 1839. To this union were born two children, Percy M., born Oct. 12, 1876, and Olive L., born Nov. 18, 1878. Mr. Purvas has served the people of his township as township treasurer, and is considered one of the well-to-do farmers of the county.

Putman, William H., a well-known resident of Durand, Mich., was born in Ovid township, Clinton county, this State, March 21, 1845. When eight years old, his parents came to Sciota township, Shiawassee county, and located on a farm, where our subject remained until 1867. In that year he removed to Vernon township and engaged in the lumber trade which he followed in this and adjoining counties for some years. In 1875 Mr. Putman succeeded in having established a post-office at Vernon Center, which was named in honor of George H. Durand of Flint, Mr. Putman being appointed postmaster the following May, serving as such for some years. In 1877 he erected a hardware store in Durand, following this business and that of buying grain and produce until 1887, when he retired from active business. Mr. Putman has served the people as township clerk and township treasurer and also one term as justice of the peace. He is now doing an extensive insurance business and represents some of the best insurance companies in the country. He was united in marriage to Josephine M. De Lano, Aug. 13, 1872, who was a native of Wayne county, N. Y. To this union have been born two children, a son and a daughter.

Pulver, Henry H., attorney at law of Laingsburg, was born in Livingston county, N. Y., Sept. 4, 1843. He came from Penneyan, N. Y., to Shiawassee county, Mich., in 1851. On the breaking out of the war, he enlisted Aug. 11, 1861, in company E, 8th Michigan Infantry, and served with that organization and the U. S. Engineer corps, until June 29, 1865. The following summer he began the study of law in the office of Col. E. Gould at Owosso, and was admitted to the bar in 1866. Mr. Pulver became a resident of Laingsburg in 1877, and has practiced his profession at this place since that time. In 1884 he was elected to the State senate and has also served the people of Laingsburg, as president of the village and village attorney for the past ten years. He has been successful in the practice of law and enjoys a large business.

Post, Hiram M., the leading hardware dealer of Owosso, is a native of this county, having been born in the village of Shiawassee June 9, 1850. He received his education in the schools of the county, and at an early age learned the tinner's trade. At the age of eighteen he moved to Vernon, and engaged in the grocery trade as clerk, which business he followed for some years, there and at Fowlerville, Mich. Later, however, he began to work at his trade, which he followed in different

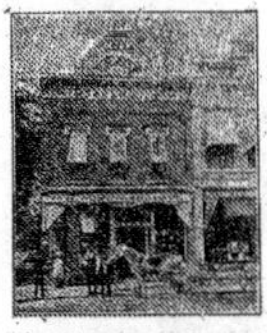

places throughout the State until 1885, when he came to Owosso and founded his present business, where he now carries a complete line of shelf and heavy hardware. Mr. Post is a competent tinner, and makes a specialty of eavestroughing and tin and steel roofing. He has served the people as alderman from the first ward, and in that capacity has given complete satisfaction to the entire city. Mr. Post was married Feb. 22, 1871, to Miss Ida Ching. To this union have been born two children, Ernest H. and Cecil O.

Reazin, B. M., *a well-to-do farmer of Shiawassee* county, was born near Quebec, Canada, Sept. 30, 1845. He was educated in the schools of Cleveland, Ohio, and in 1868 came to Michigan. He followed the occupation of a farm laborer until 1885, when he purchased the farm he now owns. Mr. Reazin was married Aug. 14, 1873, to Miss Emily Fales, who was also a native of Canada. He and his wife are members of the Congregational Church, and are well known and highly respected throughout the township.

Reed, George W., a farmer of Vernon township, was born at Dryden, Tompkins Co., N. Y., Sept. 20, 1832. He came to Michigan in 1836 and located on a farm which he now owns. The father of our subject, Mr. W. K. Reed, was born in Bucks county, Pennsylvania, June 2, 1794. He participated in the war of 1812, and was wounded at the battle of Fort Niagara. He came to Michigan in 1836 and died here March 26, 1868; his wife dying the following year, May 4, 1869. Our subject, Mr. George W. Reed, was married Jan. 1, 1861, to Miss Eliza L. Randolph, a native of Bradford county, Pennsylvania. To this union have been born six children, four of whom are now living. Mr. and Mrs. Reed are among the oldest settlers of Shiawassee county and during their many years residence have made many warm friends throughout the township.

Reed, John, The subject of this mention is one of Vernon township's oldest and most highly respected citizens. He was born at Ithica, N. Y., in 1820. When three years of age his parents moved to Dryden, N. Y., where he received his early education. In 1836 his family came to Michigan and located on the farm now occupied by his brother, George Reed, in this township. Mr. Reed soon began purchasing land in small quantities and is now the possessor of a farm containing one hundred and fifty-seven acres, which is considered one of the best in the county. He was united in marriage July 3, 1845, to Miss Mary A. Mc Collum, also a native of New York State. They are the parents of six children, two of whom are now living. Mr. Reed has by industry and economy secured for himself and family not only one of the best homes in the county, but a sufficient quantity of this world's goods to provide for them in their old age. They have also made many warm friends, and are highly respected by all of their acquaintances.

Reimer, Cyrus, one of the leading hardware merchants of Owosso, Mich., was born at Easton, Pa., in 1834. He came to Michigan in 1868, and first located at Rochester, where he remained for eleven years. For the next fourteen years of his life Mr. Reimer was employed as traveling salesman for the firm of Bohl Sons & Co., wholesale hardware dealers of Detroit, and traveled through Michigan, northern Indiana, and Ohio. In 1893 Mr. Reimer left the employ of this company and engaged in the retail business at Owosso in the store which he now occupies and which he had purchased two years previous. He was married in 1889 to Miss Addie Monroe, a resident of Hillsdale, Mich. Mr. Reimer is recognized as one of the live business men of Owosso and has by industry and close attention to business built up a large and profitable trade.

Reynolds, Preston B., one of Shiawassee county's best-known citizens, was born in this county, Jan. 28, 1850, and is the eldest son of Geo. M. and Mary R. Reynolds. The Reynolds family came from Vermont, and were among the pioneer settlers of central Michigan. Mr. Reynolds was united in marriage Oct. 4, 1870, to Miss Celia E. Cooper. To this union have been born three sons; Chauncy P., Feb. 13, 1875; Floyd C., Nov. 25, 1878; and Leo C., June 11, 1880. In politics Mr. Reynolds has been and is an ardent supporter of the Republican party. He and his family are members of the Maple River Baptist church. He is recognized as one of the most progressive and substantial farmers of the county.

Richardson, Frank A., farmer of Bennington township, was born in Caledonia township Aug. 14, 1865. He was united in marriage Oct. 9, 1887, to Miss Carrie E. Reynolds. To this union have been born two children, a son and a daughter. Mr. Richardson is a member of the Disciple church of Owosso, and is well known *and highly respected throughout the county.* He was a son of Merritt Richardson, one of the early settlers, who located near Owosso about forty years ago, and who did much to improve and build up the county to the time of his death in August, 1894. Mr. M. Richardson was strictly temperate, a man of high moral character, and who believed in following the "golden rule." He was a respected member of the community in which he lived.

Roth, Paul M., the leading merchant tailor and hatter of Owosso, was born in Ionia, Mich., in 1860. He remained in Ionia until 1876, when he moved to Saginaw where he learned the tailor's trade, and later that of the cutter's in Chicago. In 1881 Mr. Roth came to Owosso and entered the employ of Mr. Mc Bain, the *present post-master,* with whom he remained for two years. At that time he engaged in business for himself on a small scale, which he has enlarged from time to time until at the present time he is running the leading establishment of Owosso. He was married in 1891, to Miss Irah M. Black, daughter of George R. Black, a prominent dry-goods merchant of this city. Mr. Roth is at present senior major of the third regiment, Michigan National guards, and also captain of the uniform rank, Knights of Pythias. He has been more than ordinarily successful in business, and his trade extends through this and adjoining counties.

Robinson, Charles O., liveryman at Morrice, Mich., was born in Bennington township, Mar. 26, 1866. He was educated in the common schools of the county, and in Devlin's Business College at Bay City. Mr. Robinson has been engaged in the livery business since November, 1893, and has a well-equipped stable at Morrice, where he is now doing a profitable business.

Ruggles, Fred S., M. D., physician and surgeon of Byron, Mich., was born in the State of Vermont in 1856. Dr. Ruggles continued to reside in his native State until twenty-three years of age, when he came to Ann Arbor, Mich., to enter the medical department of the university, graduating from there in 1881. He first began to practice his profession at Flint, where he remained one year, when he removed to Byron and has *practiced here since that time.* He was married in 1883 to Miss Effie A. Knapp, a resident of Washtenaw county, Michigan. To this union has been born one child, Agnes M. In politics Dr. Ruggles is a Republican and has served several terms as president of the village. He has been unusually successful in the practice of his profession, and enjoys a large practice in the village and throughout the country.

Rush, Frank H., farmer of Owosso township, was born in Bennington township, this county, Jan. 20, 1858; was educated in the common schools of the county, and has followed farming as an occupation through life. September 18, 1880, he was united in marriage to Miss Cora Matlock, a native of Canada, who was born Aug. 1, 1857. To this union have been born three children. Mr. Rush carries on a general farming business, and is the owner of eighty acres of good farm land on section 35, Owosso township. He has served the people of his township as town clerk and in other official capacities.

Ryon, Austin, a farmer of Sciota township, was born in Calhoun county, Michigan, in 1846, and continued to reside in that county until nine years of age. His parents then moved to Shiawassee county where he has since resided. Mr. Ryon is the owner of one hundred and thirty acres of good land which is all under a high state of cultivation. He was elected to the office of drain commissioner, the duties of which he has discharged in a manner that reflects great credit on himself. He was married in 1871 to Miss Catherine Kief. Mr. Ryon is recognized as one of the successful farmers of Shiawassee county, where he enjoys a large acquaintance.

Schoch, William, farmer of Venice township, was born in Northampton county, Pa., in 1837. He continued to reside in his native State until twenty-one years of age, and moved to Oakland county, Mich., and resided there until 1880. In that year he moved to Venice township, this county, and purchased the farm on which he now resides. He has been twice married. His second marriage occurred in 1872 to Catherine Weller. To this union have been born two daughters. Mr. Schoch possesses one of the best farms in Shiawassee county, which is under a high state of cultivation. His home is one of the most pleasant in the county, and he and family are well known throughout the township.

Scott, E. H., M. D., a well known physician and surgeon of Laingsburg, was born in the Dominion of Canada, Dec. 9, 1859. The early years of his life were spent near Peterborough, Canada, and he later moved to Essex county, where he engaged in the mercantile business which he successfully operated for eight years. Dr. Scott entered the Detroit Medical College in 1891, and graduated from there in 1894. He began the practice of his profession at Laingsburg the same year, and has successfully followed it since that time. He was united in marriage to Miss E. E. Hill, in 1882. To this union has been born one child, a daughter. Dr. Scott has been more than successful as a medical practitioner, and enjoys a large business in Laingsburg and the adjoining county.

Schautz, Chris, a farmer of New Haven township, was born in Wurtemberg, Germany, Jan. 29, 1851. He emigrated to America in 1853, and came to Shiawassee county in 1854. He was married Jan. 1, 1881 to Miss Mary Kurrle. To this union have been born two children, one son and a daughter. Mr. Schautz has greatly improved his farm, and has it all under a high state of cultivation.

Schautz, Fred, *a farmer of New Haven township,* was born at Wurtemberg, Germany, May 4, 1840. He came to the United States in 1853, and first located in Buffalo, N. Y., where he remained for a short time, moving from there to Genesee county, Mich., and from the latter place to this county in 1860. He was married July 3, 1864, to Miss Amanda T. Dumond. To this union have been born five children, two sons and three daughters. Mr. Schautz has served the people of New Haven township as treasurer for two years, drain commissioner two years, and in other official capacities. He is well known throughout the township and highly respected by all.

Schautz, John, farmer of New Haven township, was born in Wurtemberg, Germany, March 16, 1843. He came to the United States in 1853, and to the State of Michigan in 1854. During the late war, he served as a member of company I, 8th Michigan Infantry, for three years and eleven months. He was twice wounded, and saw much active service. He was united in marriage, Oct. 18, 1868, to Miss Sellina Linzey. To this union have been born four children, two sons and two daughters. One son and one daughter are dead. Mr. Schautz is considered one of the well-to-do farmers of New Haven township, and the farm which he now owns has been their home for the past twenty-six years.

Seizer, George, the leading butcher of Corunna, was born in Wurtemberg, Germany, Oct. 10, 1853. He was educated in the schools of his native land and remained there until 1883. That year he emigrated to America and came direct to Owosso, where he remained for two years, moving from there to Corunna where he

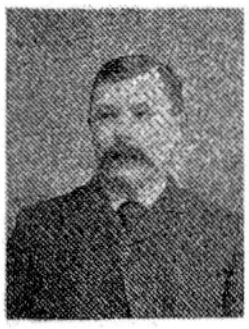

established his present line of business. He was married to Miss Bertha Timp, also a native of Germany, *who came to this country in 1883. To this union have* been born four children, three of whom are now living. Since engaging in business at Corunna, Mr. Seizer has built up a large trade, and always has on hand a large assortment of the choicest meats.

Scougale, Munroe L., ex-postmaster at Durand, Mich., and the senior member of the grocery firm of Scougale & Barlow, is one of Durand's best-known citizens. He was born Dec. 15, 1853, on a farm which is now the site of the village of Durand. At the age of sixteen, Mr. Scougale learned the carpenter's and joiner's trade, and became very proficient in that business. He was married Feb. 3, 1875, to Mary A. Grumley. Six children have been born to them, three of whom are now living. Mr. Scougale has always taken an active interest in public affairs, and has been chosen by the people to fill many responsible public positions, having served two terms as justice of the peace, resigning that office in May, 1889, to accept the position of postmaster at Durand, the duties of which office he ably discharged until 1893. In the spring of 1890 he was elected assessor for the village and is still serving in that capacity. In 1893 he was elected supervisor for Vernon township and re-elected for the term of 1894 and 1895. For many years he has been an active member of the school board, and during his entire service as a public official, he has so discharged the duties of the different offices to which he has been elected as to give entire satisfaction to the people of his town and county.

Shannon, Amymour E., merchant and farmer of Carland, Mich., was born in the village of Reading, Hillsdale Co., Mich., June 11, 1861. He came with his mother to Shiawassee county, when nine years of age, and located on part of the farm which he now owns. In 1885 Mr. Shannon organized the firm of Shannon & Banghart which did a general merchandising business for some time. At the end of one year he purchased the entire business, and conducted it until 1889, when he disposed of it. In 1890 however, he bought the entire stock in company with Mr. Park Scott, and is now doing a general business under the firm name of Shannon & Scott. They carry a general line of gro-

PORTRAITS AND RESIDENCE OF JOHN REED AND WIFE,
VERNON TOWNSHIP.

THE LENNON ELEVATOR, PROPERTY OF GEO. F. BEAHAN, LENNON.

RESIDENCE OF MRS. JANE WHITE, VERNON TOWNSHIP.

ceries, dry goods, boots and shoes, farm implements, and sell the famous Osborn binder. Mr. Shannon was married April 21, 1882, to Miss Libbie Sherburn. To them have been born six children, five of whom are now living. In 1889 Mr. Shannon was elected supervisor of the township and served for two years. He has also served a number of years as a member of the school board, and has been notary public for a number of years.

Sherman, Horace, a farmer of Hazelton township, was born at Dearborn, Wayne Co., Mich., Dec. 25, 1844. When quite young he learned the carpenter's trade, which he followed for ten years, and later engaged in farming. In 1885 Mr. Sherman came to Hazelton township and purchased the farm on which he now resides. He was united in marriage June 10, 1868, to Miss Elizabeth Hadley, a native of England. To this union have been born six children, four of whom are now living. Mr. Sherman has served the people of his township as justice of the peace and enjoys the respect and confidence of all who know him.

Sherman, Mrs. Rhoda L., is a well known resident of Byron. She was born in Marcellus, Onondaga Co., N. Y., in 1823, and is a daughter of Adam Dunlap, who was a well-known citizen of that county. She was first married in 1840 to Orange Comstock, whose death occurred in 1858. To this union were born six children; viz., George, now residing in Kansas; Martin, deceased; Francis, deceased; Martin D., who is now a resident of Byron, where he is engaged in the hardware business; Eugene, who died in the service of his country, at the age of eighteen years; and Adelia, now Mrs. Haight. Mrs. Comstock was again married in 1860, to John Lowry, a resident of Michigan, and with him came to this State. They first located on a farm at Lodi Plains, Michigan, and afterward lived in the village of Saline, from which they came to Shiawassee county and purchased a farm in Burns township. Here Mr. Lowry died in 1872. In 1873 Mrs. Lowry was united in marriage to Mr. B. P. Sherman, a prosperous farmer of Livingstone county. They removed to Bancroft and resided there until Mr. Sherman's death in 1883. In 1893 she came to Byron, where she now resides. Mrs. Sherman has led an active life and has always taken a deep interest in public affairs, and during the war assisted in every way the Union cause. She is a member of the M. E. Church, and is one of its most active workers.

Shiawassee County Bank. The above named banking firm was organized under the banking laws of Michigan, at Durand, Oct. 6, 1891, with a capital of $25,000, and its present officers are the following gentlemen: President, W. H. Clark; vice-president, C. H. Sayre; cashier, F. N. Conn. They do a general banking business, paying four per cent interest on time deposits, and enjoy the confidence of the people of Durand and vicinity.

Shipman, Charles W., farmer of Venice township, was born in Niagara county, N. Y., Nov. 1, 1848. He came with his parents to Michigan in 1853, and in the following year settled on a farm in Venice township which he now owns. He was united in marriage in 1873 to Miss Mary J. Emory, who was born in Niagara county, N. Y., Aug. 7, 1852. To this union have been born four children, Clark W., Sidney J., Celia H., and Seymour. Mr. Shipman is one of the well-to-do farmers of this township, and his farm is under a high state of cultivation.

Simonson & Son, exclusive dealers in gent's furnishing goods, clothing, etc., of Bancroft. Mr. W. F. Simonson, the senior member of the firm, was born at Birmingham, Oakland Co., Mich., June 17, 1841. He has been engaged in business the greater part of his life and for a number of years was a member of the firm of J. L. Simonson & Company of Bancroft, and later engaged in the insurance and real estate business. In 1892 in company with his son, James C., he founded their present business. They carry a complete stock, and have built up a large trade in Bancroft and throughout the surrounding country.

Smith, Hon. Stearns F., of the city of Owosso, was born near Cleveland, Ohio, Sept. 18, 1835. In 1853 he came with his parents, Elijah T. and Caroline Smith, to Perry, in this county. In 1855 he returned to Ohio, where he remained until the spring of 1859, when he emigrated to the Pacific coast, remaining there until December, 1866. He then returned to Perry, residing there, at Saginaw, and in Williamston, Ingham county, until 1878, when he removed to Owosso. He was married to Ellen F. Scofield, of Locke, Ingham county, in 1867. They have two children, viz., Grace, unmarried, and Mrs. Fred Edwards, of Owosso. Mr. Smith is a prominent lawyer, actively engaged in the practice of his profession. During his residence in Owosso, he has held the offices of supervisor, city attorney, and mayor; also the office of prosecuting attorney of Shiawassee county.

Smith, J. L., M. D. This well-known physician and surgeon of Vernon was born in Coshocton county, Ohio, in 1845. He first began the study of medicine in 1866, at Millersburg, Ohio, and completed the same by a course in Cleveland, at the University of Wooster, graduating from the medical department of that institution. Dr. Smith came to Vernon in 1875, and has successfully practiced his profession in this place since that time. His practice extends throughout the entire county, and he is recognized as one of the most thorough physicians and surgeons in this part of the State.

Small, James H., farmer of New Haven township, was born in Canada, June 10, 1856. He came to Michigan in 1872 and first settled in Ingham county, residing there for two years. In 1874 he came to Shiawassee county and settled in New Haven township, where he has since resided. He was united in marriage Jan. 1, 1884, to Miss Etta M. Thompson, who was born in Lawrence, Mass., July 30, 1859. To this union have been born five children, one son and four daughters. Mr. Small is one of the well-known farmers of New Haven township, and is at present serving the people as road commissioner of that township.

Stone & De Vore, proprietors of the two city meat markets of Durand, situated on Saginaw and Main streets, respectively. These gentlemen have been engaged in this business for the past two years, and have also been extensively engaged in buying and shipping stock. They carry a complete line of fresh and salt meats, and are thoroughly conversant with their business in all its departments. They have by strict attention to business built up a large trade in the village and throughout the adjoining country.

Sites, Gustave, this well-known dentist of Durand, was born in the town of Manslaw, Poland, March 15, 1817. He was educated in the schools of his native land and served twelve years as a member of the standing army in that country. In July, 1849, Mr. Sites

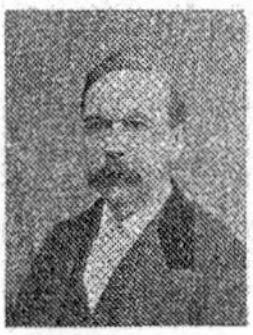

came to America and first settled at New London, Conn., and there learned the dentist's trade, which he has followed through life. He is now located at Durand, and is doing a large and profitable business.

Sleeth, James, the editor and proprietor of the *Byron Herald*, is a native of Monaghan county, Ireland, from which country he emigrated with his parents in 1838. They settled in Oakland county, Michigan, where his parents resided until their death. He graduated in medicine at Hudson, Ohio, in 1856, and followed his profession at Byron until 1870; in that year he was appointed postmaster and served as such for eight years. In 1885 he founded the *Byron Herald*, which he is still editing. He is also a member of the bar and pays some attention to legal business. During the late war, Mr. Sleeth served as assistant surgeon of the 6th Michigan cavalry, being discharged at Fort Laramie, Wy., in 1865. The *Herald* is a very newsy sheet, non-partisan in politics, and enjoys a wide circulation.

Sprague, Otto L., the leading druggist of Owosso, is a native of this State, having been born in Farmington, Oakland county, Jan. 19, 1865. When Mr. Sprague was seven years old, his parents moved to Caro, Mich., where he received his education, graduating from the high school of that place in 1882. He soon procured a position in the drug store of that place, and a year later entered business at Fair Grove, conducting a branch store at Bad Axe. In 1886 he removed to Owosso, having disposed of his business both at Fair Grove and Bad Axe, and shortly afterward found employment at Traverse City, remaining there three years, resigning his position in that place to assume the management of the drug business of M. A. Sprague & Co., of Owosso. Mr. Sprague was married July 23, 1886, to Miss Mabel Atwood of Caro, Mich. To this union have been born two children; one child, a son, is living. In politics Mr. Sprague is an ardent Republican and was elected on that ticket to the office of city clerk in the spring of 1894, and to the office of city treasurer in 1895, the duties of which he is now discharging.

Southworth, Silas B., a well known resident of Middlebury township, was born in Cayuga county, N. Y., April 10, 1830. He came to Hillsdale, Mich., in 1853, and resided there for two years, moving from there to Clinton county in 1855. During the late war, Mr. Southworth enlisted on the 23rd of December, 1863, and served until Jan. 28, 1865, when he was discharged for disabilities on account of a wound he received at the battle of Cold Harbor. He returned to his home in Clinton county, and in the fall of 1867 came to Shiawassee county and settled in Middlebury township, where he has since resided. He was married Sept. 17, 1852, to Miss Elizabeth Soule. To this union has been born one child, a son.

Stoddard, Hiram D., the popular merchant of Judd's Corners, was born in Washtenaw county, Mich., Nov. 28, 1853. He came to Hazelton township in April, 1889 and has been engaged in business at Judd's Corners since that time. Mr. Stoddard was united in marriage Dec. 8, 1875, to Miss Sarah B. Ford. To this union have been born two children, both of whom are living. He carries a complete stock of groceries, dry goods, boots and shoes, and everything else that can be found in a strictly first-class store. His business has steadily increased, and he now enjoys a large trade throughout this and adjoining townships.

Strong, Arthur P., farmer of Bennington township, was born in Prince Edward Isle, April 15, 1864. He joined his parents in Michigan when ten years of age, and received his education in the common schools of this State. He followed the occupation of a clerk eleven years, since which time he has been engaged in farming in Bennington township. He was united in marriage Sept. 17, 1891, to Miss Leora Curtis. He and wife have a pleasant home in Bennington township and have many acquaintances throughout the county. Mr. Strong is now serving the people as township clerk, and is so discharging the duties of that office as to reflect great credit on himself.

Studevant, William, the genial proprietor of the Exchange hotel, is a native of Vermont, having been born there in 1855. At the age of ten years he came with his parents to Michigan, and first located at Plainfield. In 1868 he came to Owosso with his brother, and attended the schools of this city. In July, 1894, in company with his brother, H. B. Studevant, he purchased the Exchange Hotel, which is a modern thirty-two-roomed and steam-heated house. These gentlemen have improved it in many ways and it is to-day one of the best two-dollar-a-day houses in the State.

Stewart, Hiram, farmer of Venice township, was born in Madison county, New York, Dec. 13, 1853. He resided there until 1866, when he removed to the State of Illinois and remained there until 1867, coming to this county in 1870. He was married in 1875 to Miss Mary E. Martin, a resident of Corunna, Mich. Mr. Stewart follows general farming, but has given special attention to the breeding of horses and sheep, and now owns some of the best in the county. His farm is under a high state of cultivation, and he is recognized as one of the thrifty and enterprising farmers in the county.

Swarthout, Edson, of Sciota township, is recognized as one of the most thrifty farmers in Shiawassee county. He owns a beautiful farm of two hundred acres on section 4 of this township, which is under the highest state of cultivation. His home is one of the most modern in the county, and his barns cover over five hundred feet of surface. Mr. Swarthout is well known in Sciota township, and his opinion on matters pertaining to the farm is held in high esteem by his neighbors.

Thomas, A. S., the genial proprietor of the Durand Junction House, was born at Chatham, Ont., July 25, 1853. He came to Michigan in 1860, and first located in Detroit, moving from there to Owosso in 1871. May 17, 1887, Mr. Thomas came to Durand and assumed the business which he is now conducting. The hotel is one of the best on the line of the C. & G. T., D. G. H. & M., T. A. A. & N., and C. S. & M. railroads. Besides conducting a first-class hotel, he has also established for the convenience of the traveling public a neat and tasty lunch-counter in connection with the house.

Thomas, C. H., farmer of Bennington township, was born at Nelson, Madison Co., N. Y., June 23, 1829. He removed with his parents to Wyoming county, N. Y., in 1835, and from there to Shiawassee county, Michigan, in June, 1866. He was united in marriage Sept. 7, 1854, to Miss Almira Trall, a native of Allegheny, county, New York. To this union were born three children, two of whom are now living. During the late war, Mr. Thomas served as a member of Company F, 10th N. Y. Volunteers, serving from December 1861 to July 1865. Mr. Thomas has followed farming as an occupation through life, and now owns one of the best improved farms in Shiawassee county.

Thompson, Frank A., farmer of Caledonia township, was born in that township, June 21, 1864. He has followed farming as an occupation through life, and now owns the old homestead where he was born. He was united in marriage to Miss Ella M. McGaw, Sept. 1, 1887. To this union has been born one child, who is now living. Besides carrying on general farming Mr. Thompson has been extensively engaged in the breeding of Jersey cattle, and now has at the head of his herd the celebrated bull, Gold Dust No. 39294. He has been unusually successful in this department, and is one of the well-known breeders of the State.

Thompson, William L., dealer in agricultural implements at New Lothrop, was born at Pontiac, Mich., Oct. 3, 1872. Mr. Thompson came to New Lothrop in 1883, and followed the carpenter's trade at this place for eight years. He then began the sale of agricultural implements, and has added to his stock from time to time till it is now the most complete in the county. He handles the celebrated Deering binders and mowers, the Gale plow, the D. M. Osborn harrows and horse rakes, and a full line of repairs. Mr. Thompson's success in business has been due to the fact that he has always given it his whole and undivided attention, and that the class of goods that he handles is all that he claims them to be.

Topping, James L., a member of the Shiawassee bar, was born at the town of Mentz, Cayuga Co., N. Y., Jan. 10, 1825. He came with his parents to Michigan at the age of seven years, they locating on a farm near Ann Arbor, where they remained until 1833. They subsequently moved to Livingston county, where our subject remained until he was twenty-two years of age. He then went to Bergen county, New Jersey, and there taught school for one year. He afterward returned to Michigan and learned the trade of a carpenter and joiner which he followed for some years.

He began the study of law and was admitted to the Genesee county bar in 1858, and practiced his profession in that county until 1862, when he entered the service of his country as Lieutenant of company I, 16th Michigan Infantry. He was wounded at the battle of Fredericksburg, and compelled to resign in May, 1863. He returned to Michigan and again took up the practice of law, which he followed at Fenton until 1889. In that year he came to Shiawassee county, and settled at Corunna, where he resided until 1891. He then came to Owosso, where he has since resided. He was married in 1855 to Miss Helen C. Wixon, daughter of Dr. Wixon of Genesee County. Mr. Topping has held a number of official positions, among which can be mentioned justice of the peace, supervisor, city attorney of Fenton, and township clerk for a number of years.

Thorn, J. H., produce and commission merchant of Owosso, Mich., was born in Onondaga county, N. Y., in 1843. At the age of twenty-six Mr. Thorn came with his parents to Owosso, but soon returned to his native State where he engaged in contracting and building for sixteen years. In 1884 he returned to Owosso and here followed contracting until 1887. At that time he entered the employ of the Estey Manufacturing Co., and remained with them until 1892, when he opened his present business which he is now successfully operating. Mr. Thorn has been twice married, first in 1872 to Miss Maggie Murray, who died in 1884, leaving four children. In 1891 Mr. Thorn was again married to Miss Ester Laffingwell, a resident of this city. Mr. Thorn is recognized as one of Owosso's leading business men, and is conducting a large and profitable business.

Travis, R. E., president of the Owosso Electric Co., is a well-known citizen of this place. This company was organized in 1890. Its officers consist of the following named gentlemen: R. E. Travis, president; C. C. Travis, vice-president; C. F. Travis, secretary and treasurer; and John F. Maier, chief engineer. The plant was erected the same year of the organization of the company, and located on the river bank opposite Detroit street. It is supplied with two one hundred and fifty horse power engines, and has a capacity of one hundred and fifty arc lamps and fifteen hundred incandescents.

Turner, Josiah, Jr., was born in 1813 at New Haven Mills, about five miles from Middlebury, Vt. He was a miller by trade and long and favorably known, operating the New Haven Mills. His father's brother, Bates Turner, of St. Albans, Vt., was for many years the leading lawyer in that State, and as a matter of history, was employed by Maria Monck to prosecute certain monasteries in Canada.

The subject of this sketch studied law with his uncle, Bates Turner, at St. Albans, and graduated in a class, famous for having among its members Judge Aldis, afterward judge of the Court of Claims at Washington, and Levi Vilas, father of Senator Vilas, of Wisconsin. He married Evelyn E. Ellsworth, daughter of Dr. Ellsworth, of Berkshire, Vt., and shortly after his marriage moved, in 1839, to the then new State of Michigan. The first place at which he stopped was Ann Arbor, where he remained for a few months and then moved to Howell, in Livingston county, at which place he lived twenty or twenty-five years, holding the offices of justice of the peace, treasurer, county clerk, county judge under the old county court system, judge of probate, and afterward circuit judge, by virtue of which office he became one of the judges of the supreme court of this State. He held the judicial office for twenty-six years, or one year more than a quarter of a century. He was afterward appointed by President Arthur, consul at Amherstburg, Canada, a post of which at that time was a mere dependency of the Windsor office, but which was made a full consulate for his benefit. This office he held for nine years, and since that time has been living at Owosso, Mich., his old home, a place to which over thirty years ago he removed from Howell for the purpose of being near the center of his judicial district, and more accessible to the counties which composed it. His grandfather was Samuel Turner, of Connecticut, who died and was buried at Sharon in that State, a man long and favorably known in the educational interests of that commonwealth.

Turner, Harry H., proprietor and editor of the *Morrice News*, was born in Northamptonshire county, Eng., in 1870. At the age of sixteen he came to America, and for a number of years was employed on the Detroit daily papers as reporter and proof-reader. In 1893 Mr. Turner came to Morrice and founded the *Morrice News*, which he is now conducting. He was married Apr. 30, 1893, to Miss Delia I. Kelsey, a resident of Byron, Mich. To this union has been born one child, a daughter, Kathleen Sophia. Mr. Turner is known as one of the enterprising newspaper men of Shiawassee county, and he has succeeded in making the *Morrice News* a bright and newsy sheet.

Van Deusen, Andrew M., farmer of Fairfield township, was born in Hinkley, Medina Co., O., July 30, 1847. He came to Fairfield township, Shiawassee county, Michigan, May 16, 1855, where he has since resided. At the breaking out of the war, Mr. Van Deusen enlisted at the age of seventeen as private, in Company E, 29th Michigan Volunteers, August 24, 1864, and participated in many important battles, among which can be mentioned Decatur, Murfreesboro, Nashville, and others. He was honorably discharged September 25, 1865. Mr. Van Deusen was married May 10, 1868, to Hattie E. Gifford, a resident of Fairfield township. Mr. Van Deusen is now serving the people as clerk of Fairfield township, and is recognized as one of the leading men of that community.

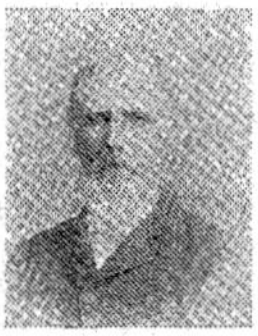

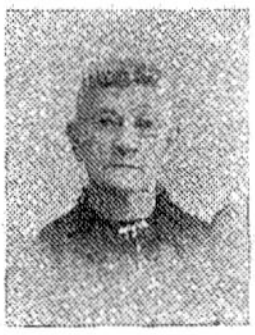

Vernon Argus, The. This paper is well known to the people of Shiawassee county, and is owned and edited by Mr. Frank Gose. Its subscription rate is $1 per year. It is published each Friday, and is bright and newsy throughout, and one of the leading papers of Shiawassee county.

Walker, C. F., a farmer of Sciota township, was born in Center county, Pennsylvania, in 1853. His parents moved from there to Niagara county, New York, when he was three years of age, and remained there until he had reached manhood. At the age of twenty he came to Clinton county, Michigan, where he remained until 1880. In that year he came to Sciota township, this county, and purchased a farm on which he now resides. He was married in Niagara county, New York, to Miss Elizabeth Wagner, daughter of Martin Wagner. Mr. Walker has served the people as school director for four years, and is well known throughout the township.

Washburn, Edwin W., the present supervisor of Fairfield township, was born in Addison county, Vermont, in 1830. Was educated in the schools of that State, and came to Michigan in 1870, purchasing the farm where he now resides. When a boy Mr. Washburn learned the trade of a tanner, and followed it for twenty-four years, eleven years of which he was in partnership with his father at Stocksborough, Vt. During the years 1868–69 he served as a member of the Legislature of Vermont, and in 1870 was elected a delegate to the Constitutional Convention of that State. Since coming to Michigan, Mr. Washburn has filled a number of official positions. In 1873 he was elected supervisor of Fairfield township, and served until 1880. He was afterward re-elected to that office, and is now discharging the duties of the same. He has also served as township treasurer and highway commissioner. Mr. Washburn was married to Miss Sarah E. Beckwith. To this union have been born two sons and one daughter, all of whom are now living.

Watson, Frank H., the present prosecuting attorney of Shiawassee county, was born in Shiawassee township, this county, in 1857. His early education was obtained in the schools of Corunna, and after graduating from the high school of that city, he at once began the study of law under the directions of Hugh McCurdy. He finished his studies under Hon. A. R. McBride, and was admitted to the bar Dec. 22, 1882. He began the practice of law at Corunna, in 1884, and followed it there until the spring of 1886, when he came to Owosso where he has since resided. Soon after coming to Owosso he formed the firm of Watson & Chapman, of which he is a senior member. Mr. Watson served as circuit court commissioner from 1884 to 1887, when he was elected to the legislature, serving the people for one term in that body. In 1890 he was appointed U. S. commissioner, and served as such for two years. In 1892 Mr. Watson was elected prosecuting attorney, and is now serving his second term in this office. During his service both as prosecutor and as a member of the legislature, Mr. Watson has given complete satisfaction. He stands in the front rank of his profession in this county, and enjoys a reputation of being possessed of more than ordinary ability. He is a member of the Masonic Fraternity and the Knights of Phythias.

Watson, Stephen, a well known farmer in Shiawassee township, was born in Durham county, England, Nov. 15, 1817. When he was but six months of age, his parents emigrated to America, and it was in the primitive schools of this country that our subject received his education. In 1850 Mr. Watson came to Michigan and located on section 8, Shiawassee township, this county, where he now owns three hundred and sixty acres of choice farming land. He was married Aug. 18, 1840, to Miss Margaret H. Kinyon, who was born in Onondaga county, New York, Jan. 24, 1821. To this union have been born six children, five sons and a daughter, all of whom are now living. Their fifth child, Frank H., is now prosecuting attorney for Shiawassee county, and a sketch of him appears elsewhere in this work. Mr. Watson is one of the early pioneers of Shiawassee county, and was among the first to hew out a home for himself and family in what was then an untrodden wilderness. He is a member of the Masonic fraternity, and enjoys the distinction of being the oldest Mason in Shiawassee county.

Waterman, J. B., farmer of Caledonia township, was born in this township Aug. 10, 1848. He was educated in the Corunna schools, and has followed farming as an occupation through life. Mr. Waterman was married Dec. 24, 1870, to Miss Lizzie Campbell, native of Wayne county, this State. To this union have been born five children, four of whom are now living. Mr. Waterman has a beautiful home, and his farm is under a high state of cultivation.

White, William H., farmer of Venice township, was born in England. Emigrated to the United States in 1870, coming direct to Venice township. For five years he followed the employment of a farm-laborer, and then purchased eighty acres of wild land on section 3, Venice township, which he has added to from time to time until he now owns one hundred and thirty acres of well-improved farm land. Mr. White has served the people as highway commissioner in 1879, as drain commissioner for 1882–'83, and has always taken a deep interest in public affairs. He carries on general farming, and is especially interested in the growing of small fruits and the breeding of Shropshire sheep. He has just commenced the erection of his new home, which is modern in every respect.

White & Whited, proprietors of the White Steam Laundry. This business was established some three years ago, and succeeded the old Pearl Laundry. The firm is composed of Messrs. H. P. White and Pitt

Whited. These gentlemen purchased the plant in 1894, and changed the name to the White Steam Laundry. They thoroughly remodeled it in every department, and are now prepared to turn out first-class work on short notice. Both of these gentlemen are well known in Owosso, and by energy and close attention to business they have built up an extensive and profitable trade.

Welch, Frank, editor of the Corunna *Journal,* and a member of the Shiawassee county bar, was born May 10, 1848 in Shiawassee county, Mich. The early years of his life were spent on the farm where he was born. He was educated in the common schools of the county, and when fourteen years of age, began clerking, which business he followed for some time, and then served as deputy county clerk for a number of years. In 1880 Mr. Welch was elected county clerk of Shiawassee county, and was re-elected to the same office three times, discharging the duties of the same until January, 1889. He was admitted to the bar in 1888, but he has never practiced. He served the people of Byron as city recorder, assessor, and trustee. Mr. Welch is at present editing the Corunna *Journal,* which is a five-column quarto, and was established in 1881. It is a reputable sheet, carefully edited, neatly printed, and has a good circulation throughout the county.

Welte, George, the popular photographer of Owosso, was born at Lansing, Mich., Sept. 26, 1857. The business which Mr. Welte is now conducting was established by Moore Bros. in 1883, and purchased by Mr. Welte in 1892. The gallery is 25 x 100 feet in area, and is supplied with the latest and most improved ap-

paratus and appliances known to art. Mr. Welte makes a specialty of cabinets, and has the reputation of doing the best work between Grand Rapids and Detroit. He enlarges portraits in crayon, india ink, pastel, and water colors. He also carries the largest stock of frames in the county. Mr. Welte is more than an ordinary photographer; he also makes view and landscape work a specialty, and does the largest business in the county in commercial and theatrical work. He is an artist of merit, and his customers come from all parts of the county. He guarantees all of his work. Parties wanting any work to their hands can feel assured that they will get a first-class job.

Wildermuth, Fred, Sr., owner and proprietor of the Wildermuth House, is a native of Germany, having been born near Stuttgart, Würtemberg, April 24, 1841. When nine years of age, his parents emigrated to America and settled at Buffalo, N. Y., and it was here that our subject was educated and learned the trade of a cooper, which he followed for a number of years. In 1863 Mr. Wildermuth came to Owosso, and in the year following accepted a position in the Exchange hotel where he remained until 1875. In that year he opened a sample room and restaurant, which he conducted until 1886, when he purchased the Wildermuth House, which he is now operating. This house is considered the leading hotel of Owosso, it is a fine three-story

brick building, heated by steam, and equipped with all the modern conveniences of a first-class hotel.

Williams, H. H., a wagon-maker and blacksmith at Bancroft, Mich., was born in the State of Ohio, and remained there until 1848, when he came to Michigan, and has been a resident of this State since that time. Mr. Williams established his present business at Bancroft in 1881, and by doing a superior grade of work has succeeded in building up a large and profitable business. He was married July 5, 1864, to Miss Delpha Donaldson. To this union have been born one child. Mr. Williams is well known in Bancroft, and has served the people of that village as president and trustee.

Williams, J. W., liveryman of Byron, Mich., is a native of this county, having been born in Burns township, Nov. 28, 1866. He was educated in the schools of the county and completed his education by a course in the Ypsilanti Business College. In 1880 his parents came to Byron and purchased a hotel, which they conducted for fifteen years, our subject assisting them during that time. In 1889 he purchased his present business which he has successfully operated since that time. He was married Oct. 8, 1890, to Miss Della Van Riper. To this union has been born one child, a daughter.

Wilkerson, Charles, farmer of Shiawassee township, was born in the State of New York, July 14, 1829. He was educated in the schools of his native State and resided there until 1862. In that year he came to Michigan and located in Shiawassee township, this county. In August of the same year he enlisted in Company H, 23d Michigan Volunteer Infantry, and served with that company until the close of the war. He participated in thirty-five battles but was fortunate enough not to be wounded. Mr. Wilkerson has been twice married, first July 7, 1852, to Miss Frances P. Johnson, who died Nov. 12, 1891. To that union was born one child. He again married Sept. 27, 1892 to Mrs. Cordelia Herriman. He and wife are pleasantly situated on a well-cultivated farm and are highly respected throughout the township.

Wilson, Sylvestus D., was born in the town of Stockbridge, Madison Co., N. Y., Jan. 8, 1842. The early years of his life were spent in farming, but at the breaking out of the war, he enlisted in Company G, 6th New York Light Artillery, Sept. 19, 1861, and served with that company until his discharge June 19, 1865. Mr. Wilson came to Michigan in April, 1881. In December 1892 he opened a meat market where he is now doing a general business in that line. He was united in marriage to Sarah E. Taber, who was born in New York State, Aug. 5, 1843. To this union have been born three children, all of whom are now living. He and wife are members of the M. E. church of New Lothrop and are highly respected by the people of that place.

Wisner, Charles H., present judge of the 7th judicial circuit of Michigan, which is composed of the counties of Genesee and Shiawassee, was born at Pontiac, Mich., Feb. 27, 1850. He is a son of Moses Wisner, who was elected governor of Michigan in 1858, and who died in the service as colonel of the 22nd Michigan Infantry. The family in America descended from Hendrick Wisner, a Swiss lieutenant in Queen Anne's army, and who came to this country in 1712. Our subject was educated in the common schools of Oakland county, and at the University of Michigan, where he graduated from the law department in the class of 1871. He at once began the practice of his profession at Flint, Mich., where he has since resided. When elected to the bench, he was a member of the law firm of Wisner, Lee & Aitken, and his late partner, Mr. Aitken, at this writing, represents the 6th district in Congress. Judge Wisner served as prosecuting attorney of Genesee county from 1882 to 1886, and has held other public positions in that county and in the city of Flint. He took his present position upon the bench Jan. 1, 1894.

Wonsey, A. B., a well-known farmer of Middlebury township, born in Livingston county, N. Y., Oct. 14, 1841. Came to Michigan and settled in Clinton county in 1854, and remained there until the break-

ing out of the war. He enlisted Dec. 5, 1863, in the 27th Michigan Cavalry, and served until May 27, 1865, when he was honorably discharged. Mr. Wonsey was married March 19, 1865, to Miss Samantha Craven, and shortly after his marriage removed to Isabella county, this State, where he resided for eleven years; he then returned to Shiawassee county, where they have resided since that time. They are the parents of twelve children, ten of whom are now living. Mr. Wonsey is well-known, and has many friends and acquaintances throughout the county.

Wood, M. and Company, This company is engaged in the manufacture of hickory handles at Owosso, Mich.; the business has been in existence for the past fifteen years. The company then consisted of Mr. M. Wood and Mr. D. A. Gould. Mr. Wood afterward retired from the firm; the business is now being operated by Mr. E. A. Gould, who is a well-known citizen of Owosso, having served the people for two terms and now elected for third term as mayor, and four years as alderman for the third ward. He is a director of the Owosso savings bank and interested in other enterprises of the city. This company employs from fifteen to twenty men and has an output of from fifteen thousand to twenty thousand dozen handles per year, which finds a market in all parts of the country.

Wyckoff, J. V. D., The leading hardware and agricultural dealer of Laingsburg, was born in the State of New Jersey in 1851. He moved with his parents to New York State in 1855, and from there to Woodhull township in this county in 1861. Mr. Wyckoff received his education at Phelps, N. Y., and Owosso, Mich. After he was twenty-one years of age, he acquired the machinist's trade at Phelps, N. Y., and there became acquainted with Carrie L. Dillingham, with whom he was united in marriage in 1878. They have one child, Kathryne D. For ten years Mr. Wyckoff carried on farming on his Woodhull farm, and in 1889 came to Laingsburg and established his present line of business, where he handles a complete line of hardware and farm implements. He has served the people as a member of the common council, and in other minor official capacities. He is considered one of her substantial business men, and enjoys a large trade.

Yanson, Morett, a farmer of Shiawassee county, was born in Vernon township, this county, 1862. His early life was spent on the home farm and attending the district schools of his native township. At the age of twenty-three he purchased his farm on which he now resides and which he has greatly improved by the erection of a fine house and good barns. He was married March 4, 1886, to Miss Sarah McRoberts, a native of Canada. Mr. Yanson has been very successful as a farmer and now owns and operates one of the best improved farms of the State.

Young, Albert, farmer of Caledonia township, was born in this township, Feb. 13, 1844. Was educated in the schools of Caledonia township, and has resided on section 11 for the past twenty-seven years. Mr. Young was united in marriage July 28, 1867, to Miss Phebe Eldridge, who was born in St. Lawrence county, N. Y., Nov. 18, 1850, and came with her parents to Michigan in 1867. To this union have been born four children, three of whom are now living. Mr. Young is one of the well-to-do farmers in Caledonia township and his eighty-acre farm on section 11 is one of the best improved in the country.

Zeigler, Jas. H., a well-known merchant of New Lothrop, was born at Baltimore, Md., Aug. 25, 1856. Came to New Lothrop, Mich., in 1883, and began his present business in April, 1894. Mr. Zeigler was united in marriage Nov. 20, 1894, to Miss Ida Klaty, a native of this State. Mr. Zeigler is a graduate of the public schools of Baltimore City; also of the Sadler's Bryant and Stratton Business College of the same place, and is a thorough business man in every way. His stock is complete in each department and he carries a full line of dry goods, groceries, boots and shoes, crockery, and wall paper. He has by energy and close attention to business built up a good trade.

CPSIA information can be obtained
at www.ICGtesting.com
Printed in the USA
BVHW031050110822
644347BV00008B/583